FOOD SCARCITY AND FAMINE:
Assessment and Response

Helen Young

Oxfam Practical Health Guide No.7

A catalogue record for this book is available from the British Library.

ISBN 0 85598 145 8   Pb
ISBN 0 85598 144 X Hb

Published by Oxfam
274 Banbury Road, Oxford OX2 7DZ
Printed at Alden Press Limited,
Oxford and Northampton, Great Britain
OX:1122DH91

CONTENTS

ACKNOWLEDGEMENTS

There are many people who have contributed in one way or another to this book. There are those, however, who deserve special mention, as without their help, advice and support it would not have been completed. In particular I would like to thank all the staff of the Oxfam Health Unit, especially Pat Diskett, and also the staff of Oxfam and Save the Children Fund in Darfur, West Sudan in 1988 and 1989. Many thanks also to John Mitchell and Hugo Slim for their comments and encouragement and to Felicity Young for the drawings and hand written tables.

Helen Young
February 1992

INTRODUCTION

The purpose of this manual is to give practical advice to staff of agencies, particularly non-governmental organisations (NGOs), who are faced with situations where food scarcity or famine have become a threat to people's livelihood and survival.

The advice in the manual is based on the experience of Oxfam and other similar agencies with relief programmes in North and East Africa. The manual aims to help field workers to make better assessments and so judge which types of interventions might be helpful. It is intended for nutritionists and non-nutritionists working in situations of food scarcity or famine. In the case of Oxfam, this might include local country representatives and their deputies, development project officers, health workers and relief staff.

The manual describes approaches to the assessment and response to a situation of food scarcity and famine and the various options involved. Assessment starts with a preliminary review of existing information, such as early warning reports or other reports from government and non-governmental agencies. This may be followed by field visits by people who know the area well and are able to make a rapid assessment. Meeting and talking with local people, both men and women, is vital in order to learn their views about the situation and also about possible interventions.

If the food crisis appears serious it may be necessary to undertake a nutrition survey to estimate the prevalence of malnutrition. Nutrition data can be very useful but, unless the survey is properly carried out, the data is likely to be unreliable. Thus, nutrition surveys should only be attempted if there is the necessary expertise available to design and carry out the survey, and if there are adequate resources and time available.

Information collected during the assessment is used to analyse the severity and nature of the situation: is it normal for the time of year, or is food scarcity threatening people's livelihoods? Are there epidemics and are more people dying than usual? Knowledge of the underlying causes of food scarcity and famine will help pin-point the appropriate actions, for example, famine-related interventions aimed at reducing excess mortality or strategies aimed at supporting people's livelihoods and avoiding epidemics by protecting health and nutrition.

Free food distribution is only one of several strategies that may be needed in response to food scarcity and famine. There are many practical difficulties to be addressed in food distribution, and in the past, food has at times failed to reach those who really needed it most. Targeting any type of programme requires information about who are most in need, where they are, and how their way of life affects efforts to reach them.

Food assistance should be considered in terms of its nutritional contribution to the diet and also its economic value to the household. This is important, especially when deciding what the composition of a food ration should be. Supplementary and therapeutic feeding are two direct nutrition interventions intended to rehabilitate malnourished children by means of both feeding and health care.

Part One of the manual discusses the nature of food scarcity and famine, what is meant by malnutrition, its causes and how it can be measured.

Part Two of the manual describes a variety of assessment methods, not all of which are normally associated with nutrition surveys, but important in learning about the wider 'livelihood' situation.

Part Three describes how to link your findings with decision making and stresses the importance of combined strategies in order to prevent excess mortality, protect health and support livelihoods. In times of famine, the immediate cause of most deaths is disease, the severity and duration of which is affected by malnutrition. Measures to protect health and avoid epidemics are therefore a priority.

The obvious response to famine is food relief, but remember 'by itself food may not be enough to change the situation but without food other interventions might fail'.* Part Four of the manual describes different types of food distribution.

The Appendices contain detailed information about survey techniques, vitamin and mineral deficiencies, nutritional information on foods used in feeding programmes, and some recipes for supplementary food mixes.

---

* G.H.Beaton (1989) *Small but healthy? Are we asking the right question?* Human Organization 48 (1) 30–39.

PART ONE

FOOD SCARCITY, FAMINE AND MALNUTRITION

In the first section of this first part of the book, we look at what is meant by the terms food scarcity and famine. Section 1.2 defines malnutrition and explains how it can be measured and some possible causes. The final section reminds the reader of the importance of taking a wider view of any situation where food scarcity seems to be a problem.

1.1 Food scarcity and famine*

People in many parts of Africa often experience difficult or 'lean' periods during the year when food is in short supply. This may be just before the harvest when last year's grain stores are nearly finished and market prices are high because the next harvest is yet to come.

Most rural people have learnt to cope with this seasonal food scarcity and are able to conserve what little food they have to see them through until their next harvest is in. People dependent on livestock also experience lean periods during the year and have similar expertise in coping with them.

This kind of seasonal food scarcity is a recurring problem but may be made worse by:

● War, insecurity or armed conflicts which prevent people from carrying on their normal lives.

● Drought, floods, pests or crop disease which adversely affect the food supply or people's access to it.

The effect of food scarcity varies and depends on people's existing resources and their ability to cope or adapt. In situations of food scarcity where people are still home-based, they usually have some means of surviving and are not yet destitute. In this situation they are still able to cope to some degree but may do so by drawing heavily on their reserves and straining or even irreversibly changing their traditional way of life.

If food scarcity continues unchecked, it will slowly exhaust all people's resources. Eventually, they may become destitute and, as a last resort, be forced to leave their homes in search of work and food. In 1984 in Wollo

---

* Many of the ideas presented in this section, in particular those concerning the cause and nature of famine, are based on the work of Amartya Sen and Jean Dreze, and also Alex de Waal. The Further Reading list at the end of this book contains details of their books.

Region of Ethiopia, gatherings of destitute people by the roadside became the camps where many thousands were to die. This is famine.

Famine therefore refers to the **later stages of food scarcity** when people become destitute and many more than normal die because of the conditions produced by famines which encourage the spread of disease. High mortality during famine is much more common in camps of displaced people than among people able to stay in their own homes.

Both food scarcity and famine cause long-term damage to people's livelihoods by eroding their resources and making it difficult for them to continue their way of life as before.

Understanding people's way of life and how they acquire food is very important in assessing a food scarcity problem and in deciding on an appropriate response. Always remember to take the social situation of people into account; **the situations and roles of women and men in their communities may be very different**, and the position of women in charge of households will be different from that of women in households with an active adult male.

Common features of food scarcity

- People's entitlements to food are reduced by poor harvests, reduced availability of food for other reasons, increased market prices, loss of livestock or other resources, loss of waged labour or other sources of income.

- People's health may be threatened by low immunisation coverage, limited access to health care due to availability or cost, high rates of malnutrition, increased prevalence of disease.

Common features of famine

- People, or even whole families, are destitute and perhaps displaced from their normal homes and may be living in makeshift relief camps.

- Undernutrition may be widespread and contributing to high rates of malnutrition.

- People may be living in conditions (overcrowding, with poor water or sanitation) that contribute to increased transmission of disease and excess mortality.

1.2 Nutrition and malnutrition

The subject of nutrition is concerned with how people stay alive and well by means of food. This includes how people obtain their food and everything that influences this, and how food is used by the body and contributes to health.

In relation to food scarcity and famine, nutrition is concerned with the **process leading to hunger and malnutrition** as well as the **state of malnutrition** itself. This process includes the immediate causes of inadequate nutrition, which are associated with diet and health, as well as the less direct causes associated with 'livelihood'.

Malnutrition usually starts either with the failure of an individual to acquire enough to eat, or ill-health. Nutritional inadequacy can lead to malnutrition, which is a state in which an individual's physical functions are impaired. The focus in times of food scarcity and famine tends to be on growth failure in children, as a result of protein energy malnutrition, and also on the effects of specific micro-nutrient deficiency diseases (Appendix 7). As well as growth failure, other physical functions are affected, including resistance to disease, the ability to work, and pregnancy and lactation.

Nutrition and infection

Health and nutrition are closely linked. Deficiencies in energy, protein and vitamin A in particular, are associated with a lowering in immunity. This means that diseases, such as measles and diarrhoea, will be of potentially increased incidence, severity and duration among malnourished children.

Death rates among children who are severely malnourished are about six times greater than among those who are healthy and well nourished in the same population (and 20 to 50 times greater than the rate in rich and prosperous countries).

In addition to the effect of nutrition on disease, the presence of disease leads to further malnutrition, through malabsorption of nutrients, altered metabolism, loss of appetite and by affecting feeding practices. Thus, the relationship between malnutrition and infection is cyclical:

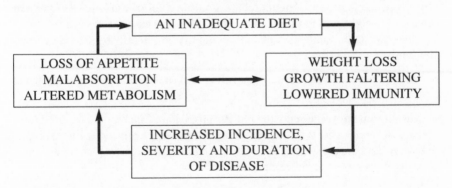

Figure 1: The malnutrition/infection cycle

(Adapted from: Tomkins, A. and F.Watson (1989), *Malnutrition and Infection, A Review*, ACC/SCN State of the Art Series, Nutrition Policy Discussion Paper No 5.)

The measurement of malnutrition

By comparing the body measurements of a child with those of healthy children of the same height or age, we can classify his or her **nutritional status**. For example, below a certain weight, a child of a specified height or age would be considered severely malnourished.

When body measurements are related to age or height in order to assess nutritional status they are known as **nutrition indices,** for example, weight for height (WFH), height for age (HFA), and weight for age (WFA). The healthy group of children that are used for comparison are known as **the reference population**. Tables 8 and 9 in Appendix 5 show the weights of children between 49cm and 130cm from the internationally accepted reference population (NCHS/ CDC/ WHO Reference Population).

Anthropometric (body) measurements are useful because anthropometry is a direct measure of an individual's nutrition and growth. Collectively, the anthropometric measurements of children may be used for comparing different populations or for making comparisons over time. Anthropometry may be used as a marker of the process that has led to individual growth failure or high rates of malnutrition in the population.

In times of food scarcity and famine, weight loss among children is a useful proxy indicator for the general health and well-being of the entire community. **Malnutrition is closely linked to conditions of poverty**, and weight loss among children in a community is strongly associated with access (entitlements) to food and health care. It is not safe to assume that everyone in the community, or each person within a family, has equal entitlements to food.

Nutrition indices have the additional advantage of being based on measurements which are relatively easy to carry out, which is not true of most other indicators of poverty or reduced entitlements. **But remember that anthropometric measurements tell you nothing about the causes of growth failure or weight loss in children or about the process that has led to it.**

There are three main uses of anthropometry in situations of food scarcity and famine:

● **One-off nutrition surveys** to assess levels of malnutrition in a population at a particular point in time (a cross-sectional survey).

● **Nutritional surveillance** – the regular provision of nutrition information for making decisions that will directly or indirectly affect nutrition. For example, nutrition data may be used for preventing food crises as part of an early warning system or for relief programme management (targeting, monitoring and evaluation).

● **Screening individuals** to identify the most severely malnourished children for targeted relief interventions, such as supplementary feeding (see page 63).

But it is not enough just to measure how many thin children there are. In addition you must find out **why** they are thin.

The causes of malnutrition

In explaining what malnutrition is, it is apparent that its immediate causes are an inadequate diet and infectious disease, but taken in isolation this is a simplistic view and is only a small part of the overall picture. Figure 2 shows how an individual child's food intake is influenced by a variety of factors within the household, for example, the total food available to the household, how that food is distributed between the household members and the actual quality of the food eaten. Gender can determine food distribution within the family, with women and girls receiving less food than men and boys.

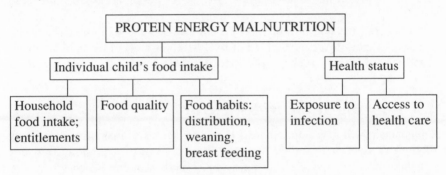

Figure 2: Direct causes of malnutrition within the household

Beyond the level of the household, in the village or region, are numerous other factors, which influence what food the household is able to obtain and household members' health, and therefore indirectly influence nutritional status (Figure 3, page 14). For example, the food system determines what food is available, while people's position in society and their livelihoods influence their access to the available food. Health, on the other hand, is affected by exposure to infection and also by people's access to health care and other basic services (clean water, sanitary facilities and education). It is not surprising, therefore, that malnutrition is closely linked with conditions of poverty.

The multiple causes of malnutrition interact in a complex way and are difficult to unravel. However, in times of food scarcity and famine, when undernutrition and malnutrition are considerably worse than in normal times, it is possible to make certain generalisations. In particular, there are two key factors which influence the food intake of the household:

● The **availability of food** in the area.

● People's access or **entitlements** to that food.

7

People's access to food is dependent on their way of life, and how they obtain their food. For example, farmers may grow much of their own food and rely on sales of food for purchases of other essential items, whereas employees are dependent on their earnings to buy food in the market place.

Food availability and people's access to food are often closely linked; a poor harvest will reduce the income of the farmer, and will also affect all those dependent on agricultural labour as a source of income. Others may be affected by the likely increases in market prices. However, these groups will probably be affected to different degrees, and this is not apparent unless people's livelihoods and subsequent entitlements are considered. If food scarcity and famine is thought of only in terms of food availability, and not entitlements to food (including the effect of gender differences in entitlements), then it is wrongly assumed that everybody is affected by food shortage to the same extent.

In general, the question of food availability is more important where the growing of crops is a major source of livelihood for most of the population, so that crop failures affect people's entitlements as well as causing food shortages.

1.3 Looking at the wider picture

This manual will help you to assess the wider causes of malnutrition in times of food scarcity and famine. It will show you ways of assessing the wider situation of people, which is so important in understanding which groups are most affected and how best to support them. The assessment methods in the next part of the book are important if you want to learn about the wider livelihood situation. They will help you to identify appropriate actions aimed at supporting people's livelihoods, and so improving their access to food.

PART TWO

ASSESSMENTS AND SURVEYS

Making an assessment is the first step towards making better and more informed decisions. What you find out during your assessment will influence your decisions about appropriate actions or interventions. Decisions need to be made about three key areas:

- The **appropriate response** or actions, if any.

- **Targeting** – ensuring that any intervention reaches the priority groups i.e. those people who need it most.

- The **agency's role** in any response.

Decisions in these three areas will depend on the findings of your assessment and the analyses of the situation. You will always be faced with some doubts and uncertainties because of the limits of your knowledge and understanding, and because the situation is likely to be constantly changing. But the understanding gained from a good assessment will give you confidence to make the right decisions.

The five main stages of making an assessment are as follows:

- **Deciding what information you need for decision making.**

- **Choosing methods of collecting the information.**

- **Planning your assessment and organising your team.**

- **Analysing and interpreting your findings.**

- **Presenting your findings.**

In this part of the book, we will look at these stages in detail. Part 2.1 looks at the three main aspects of the situation that you need to find out about: how severe it is, what has caused it and who is most affected. Part 2.2 examines in detail the different methods available for collecting the information you need. Initial assessments, rapid assessments and nutrition surveys are fully described and evaluated. Planning and organising the necessary fieldwork is covered in Part 2.3, which also deals with the selection and training of a fieldwork team. When you have carried out the assessments, you will then have to analyse the data, and make judgements about what it tells you about the situation, and this is covered in Part 2.4. Finally, Part 2.5 deals with the presentation of your findings, and how to communicate the information you have gathered to people who need to know.

2.1 Deciding what information you need for decision making

In your assessment you need to find out:

- **If there is a problem and how severe it is:** Is it a famine that is killing people or threatening to kill people? Or is it a situation of food scarcity that is damaging to people's livelihoods in the longer term? Has the situation been exaggerated and results only from expected seasonal fluctuations in the availability of food?

- **The underlying causes of the problem:** Has the situation been caused principally by food shortages or failed entitlements or a combination of both? What are the underlying causes?

- **The people who are most affected:** How are different socio-economic groups affected and whose health and livelihood is most vulnerable?

In addition, during your assessment you will need to consider the long-term effects of interventions; the logistical and administrative constraints of any intervention; the response of government and other agencies; and how the agency can support people as they adapt to the situation. These points will be discussed more fully in Part 3: Using your findings in making decisions.

Throughout the assessment there is one **golden rule**: remember to concentrate on the minimum information needs. Always ask yourself whether the information is needed for making decisions. Do not waste time and resources collecting data that is not immediately relevant.

2.1.1 Assessing the severity of the problem

Extreme food scarcity and famine eventually lead to increased malnutrition, infectious disease and death. Where these are found, emergency interventions are usually necessary.

The most dangerous situations are those where people in desperation have migrated from their homes and find themselves living in camps or squatting in urban areas in conditions that promote the spread of disease (overcrowded, insanitary, with limited or dirty water supply). The situation is often made worse by inadequate health-care facilities, or health services which are prohibitively expensive.

Information is needed about **mortality**, **morbidity**, **malnutrition** and the major **threats to health**, in order to assess how severe or life-threatening the situation is.

Mortality

Mortality is reported in a number of ways:

- **The infant mortality rate** (IMR), which is the number of infant (below one year) deaths per 1,000 live births; usually presented for a given year, but also for shorter periods if appropriate. In a rapidly changing situation it is more useful to look at deaths per 10,000 per day, averaged out over the month (per 10,000 per month). (See Table 1: The infant mortality rate in selected countries.)

- **The child death rate,** which is the number of deaths of children aged 1 through 4 years per 1,000 child population of this age per year. The child death rate usually accounts for most excess mortality.

- The **crude mortality rate**, which is the total number of deaths per 1,000 of the population per year.

Reliable mortality data is very difficult to obtain, although previous data for that area may be available from the existing health information system.

Surveys to estimate current mortality rates are generally impractical as the sample sizes needed to provide reliable estimates are very large and considerable tact and skill are needed by interviewers. It is nevertheless worthwhile bringing together whatever information has been collected, for a rough and ready indication of excess mortality. The validity of the estimate depends on the reliability of the source of mortality data and also on reliable population estimates. **Remember the extreme sensitivity of such data**.

If mortality data is not being regularly collected, a reporting system should be established, preferably as part of the health-care system. In refugee camps, surveillance of burial grounds is an improvised way of obtaining mortality data. Watchmen interview families of the deceased to find out sex, age, and cause of death.

It is useful to restrict reporting of deaths to five or six categories, for example, measles, fever (malaria), fever with cough (acute respiratory infections), diarrhoea (and dehydration), malnutrition, and other (if actual diagnosis is known). The system should allow for more than one cause of death, otherwise malnutrition may be under-reported. Grave watchers must be trained in the use of these terms, otherwise there will be some obscure diagnoses, such as 'old age', 'tiredness', 'backache'.

If actual mortality rates are unobtainable, then it is useful to look at causes of death over a specified period and try to find out if these are different from what would normally be expected at that time of year.

Infant mortality rate, deaths per 1,000 live births per year:

Ethiopia	135
Mozambique	139
Somalia	130
Uganda	101
Sudan	106
Kenya	70
Liberia	130
Tanzania	104

Source; the UN publication *Mortality of Children under Age 5: Projections, 1950 - 2025*, and also the World Bank, *World Development Report 1990*.

Peak mean monthly mortality rates in Wad Kowli refugee camp, East Sudan in 1985 (deaths per 10,000 per day, averaged for month):

Crude mortality rate	8.2	
Child mortality rate	24.8	(under 5 years)

Source; Save the Children Fund, UK.

Table 1: The infant mortality rate in selected countries

Morbidity

Even during famines, people rarely die as a direct result of malnutrition; they are killed by infectious diseases (measles, acute respiratory infections, diarrhoea, malaria). These diseases may spread more rapidly because of conditions found during famines, and also may be more severe or of longer duration because people are malnourished.

Of most immediate importance are recent or current outbreaks of disease which may be contributing to excess mortality and/or increased malnutrition. Initially, surveys to estimate the prevalence of certain diseases or symptoms are unnecessary, as decisions about treating disease or preventing its transmission may be taken without precise data. Reliable reports of actual cases and the presence of health-risk factors contributing to disease transmission are sufficient to require action.

As well as looking at clinic data, ask about what is not being reported to the clinic. For example, if there are no drugs for malaria available, people with malaria may not seek treatment and so it will be under-reported. Other diseases are also often under-reported, especially diarrhoea and malnutrition. Whether or not people report to the clinic often depends on their perceptions about the possibility of the clinic being able to help them.

Malnutrition

The prevalence of acute malnutrition among children under five years old is a proxy indicator for the health and well-being of the community. It is very unusual for rates of acute malnutrition (below 80 per cent of the reference median weight for height) to exceed 10 per cent unless communities are suffering severe stress in terms of loss of entitlements or food shortages, or have suffered an epidemic such as measles. **Prevalence of acute malnutrition above 10 per cent should be investigated further**.

Rates of malnutrition may be estimated by means of a nutrition survey (Section 2.2.3).

Threats to health

The major threats to health that contribute to the spread of infectious diseases are associated with the following factors:

- limited access to health care;

- increased exposure to infection; or

- undernutrition.

Access to health care is influenced by both the coverage and extent of health services, and also the uptake of these services. If treatment costs are prohibitively expensive, this will exclude poorer people.

Two situations in particular cause these risk factors to escalate; first is **distress migration**, which increases exposure to infection, reduces access to health care and is likely to contribute to undernutrition. The second situation is **war and insecurity**, which often prompts distress migration, but also has disastrous affects on preventive and curative health services. For example, measles immunisation coverage is often extremely poor in insecure areas.

2.1.2 Assessing the underlying causes of the problems

The introduction to this manual explained that famines are not simply a result of food shortages, but can also occur because some groups of people are unable to obtain any of the available food. In other words, they have limited access or entitlements to what food there is. People's entitlements to food vary depending on their livelihoods and position in society. Increasing the general availability of food may not help the poorest members of society, whose entitlements are inadequate.

In Africa there are many ways in which people obtain food. Figure 3 shows a flow diagram which illustrates how household food intake (entitlements) is the result of a range of possible activities, each of which is influenced by other factors. For example, household food purchases might be influenced by the source of household cash income, the availability of food in the market, the market price of foods, and how accessible the market is.

The factors shown in Figure 3 are not an exhaustive list and are only given as examples, and other activities are likely. Every situation is unique, and the interrelationship between the various factors will vary, and is likely to be complex. For example, climate and rainfall patterns affect general food availability, which will affect market prices.

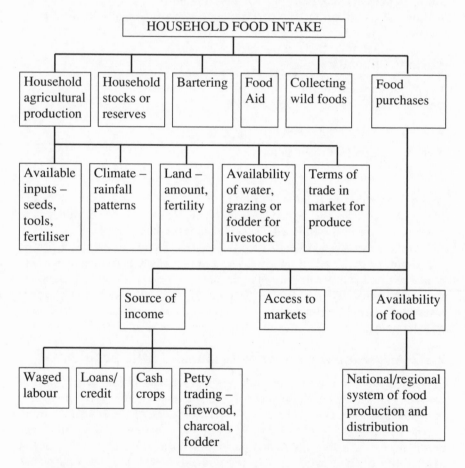

Figure 3: Factors influencing the food available to the household

People's livelihoods influence the ways in which they obtain food; pastoralists depend mostly on sale or exchange of livestock, farmers on producing and selling crops, labourers on their income. Most people in Africa rely on a combination of activities to provide themselves with food. Those who are less vulnerable to the effects of food scarcity have often developed several means of acquiring food, rather than depending on a single activity.

People's entitlements are strongly influenced by **external events** beyond their control, such as drought, war, seasonal effects of food scarcity, and government policies (market interventions, rationing, agricultural support).

Coping strategies

People will try to diversify their means of obtaining food, or money to buy food. For example, they may seek loans or gifts, gather wild foods, sell their assets such as jewellery or furniture, or undertake menial, low-status jobs they would not normally want to do, such as collecting and selling firewood. Eventually, they may leave their homes to work in other areas, or go and stay with relatives. People often go hungry by missing meals, in order to save what little food they have. This may be reflected in increasing rates of malnutrition.

2.1.3 The people who are most affected

Food scarcity and famine are likely to affect everybody in some way. For example, harvest failures often result in increased market prices, which will affect all those using the market.

However, only some groups will be threatened by loss of livelihood and destitution. You should try to distinguish between the different social and occupational groups in order to understand how they may be affected differently by food scarcity and famine. (Examples of groups who may be most vulnerable are listed in Table 2.)

Changes in people's way of life

Once the crisis is over some groups may be able to resume their previous way of life. Others may have lost the very basis of their livelihood and no longer be able to sustain a living. For example, nomads who have lost livestock, or farmers whose land is no longer productive, can no longer rely on their previous means of survival.

Rural people are adaptable and resourceful; some resettle elsewhere, others change their farming practices or livestock holdings in order to become less vulnerable 'next time round'. Changes are taking place all the time. It is important to try and **learn from rural people which strategies are most successful**. In this way, you can identify what kind of support will be most complementary to their own initiatives. **Food is not always the most useful support in situations of food scarcity**. Emergency relief programmes are potentially very disruptive to normal life and may even undermine people's traditional means of coping with food scarcity.

What is the health and nutrition situation?
Higher mortality than normal.
Outbreaks of disease.
Threats to health:

- Increased exposure to infection; overcrowding, poor quality/lack of water, inadequate sanitary facilities.

- Limited access to health care; low coverage of measles immunisation, limited provision of ORS, essential drugs, vitamin A supplementation.

- Undernutrition; rates of acute malnutrition, prevalence of micro-nutrient deficiencies.

What are the causes of the problems?

How do people normally obtain their food?
Buy from the market with cash from waged labour, loans/gifts, petty trading, sale of assets.
Household agricultural produce; livestock, food crops, household stocks.
Food aid.
Bartering.

How have recent events (e.g. drought) unusually affected access to food?
Markets; availability of food; prices (livestock, staple foods).
Harvests.
Condition of livestock, availability of water and pasture for animals.

How are people coping with or adapting to the problem of food scarcity?
Sale of assets.
Labour or distress migration.
Loans.
Support from relations or the community.
Gathering wild foods.
Increased dependence on petty trading – gathering wood or grass.

Who is most vulnerable/affected?
Those who are displaced or destitute.
Peasant farmers.
Nomads and pastoralists.
Urban poor.
Landless labourers.
Women-headed households.
The elderly.
Minority ethnic groups.
People from remote areas.

How has food scarcity and famine affected people in the past?
Previous droughts.
Previous relief programmes; lessons learnt.

How are the government, donors and other agencies responding?
What are government policies?
Existing relief and development programmes.

What future events will influence the situation?
Rains.
Harvest.
Peace agreements.
Resettlement programmes.
Development initiatives.

What is the agency's role?
Support self-help initiatives and/or other organisations.
Become operational.

Table 2: A checklist of questions to be asked

2.2 Choosing methods of collecting the information

The assessment methods available can be divided into three groups:

● **Initial assessments** review existing information or knowledge.

● **Rapid assessments** give a preliminary understanding of the situation after short visits to the area.

● **Surveys** focus on more objective measurements, such as estimates of the rate of malnutrition, or quantitative household data.

Every situation is different and so there is no single right method. You must decide where the gaps in your knowledge are and whether you can fill them with existing information (initial assessments); quick qualitative information (rapid assessments); or slower to obtain quantitative data (surveys). You may need a combination of all three.

Ideally, you should always try and use **several different ways of collecting information** from a variety of sources to get different views of the same problem. This will increase the depth of your understanding and allow you to cross-check results.

Whatever methods you use, **visit the area** itself. There is no substitute for actual field visits and talking with the people who are directly affected by food scarcity.

The most important factors which will influence your choice of assessment methods are:

- The kind of **information** you need (Section 2.1).

- How much **time** you have (Section 2.3.1).

- **People** available to be on the assessment team, and their skills and experience (Section 2.3.2).

- Other **resources** you have available (people, vehicles, fuel, money, computing facilities).

We will now look in detail at the different kinds of assessment.

2.2.1 Initial assessments

The purpose of an initial assessment is to review and summarise all the existing information and knowledge about a situation – **secondary data**. An initial assessment does not therefore collect new information.

For carrying out initial assessments, the skills of literacy, numeracy and accuracy are important. You must be thorough and seek all potential sources of information and summarise the relevant points in clear and concise notes.

The **advantages** of initial assessments are:

- They save you repeating work already done by other organisations.

- They may reveal gaps in existing knowledge, suggest what extra information is needed and stimulate ideas.

- They produce useful background information to complement your later findings.

- They suggest appropriate methods for further assessments.

The **disadvantages** of initial assessments are:

- They do not always include the views of those affected directly: there is a tendency to adopt a 'top down' approach.

- Because history does not always repeat itself, what happened in the past cannot necessarily be used to predict the future.

- The information is liable to be out of date.

Procedure for initial assessments

- Find out about the local early warning system and the contingency relief plans of government and the UN if they exist (see Appendix 1: Early warning).

- Read relevant documents and publications and talk with the 'key' people in your own and other organisations and in relevant government departments.

18

These are people who are most well-informed about the situation and likely to play an important role in subsequent relief operations.

- Summarise your findings in the form of brief notes and tables to use for future reference. A set of questions should emerge, which may form the basis of the next stage of the assessment.

- Be critical in your review of existing information. Figures and statistics may seem more 'factual' than verbal reports, but **beware**: figures are just as liable to inaccuracies and bias as verbal descriptions, and their origin should be carefully examined.

- Find out the names of local people in the area who may help you during the assessment. Letters of introduction to local people are usually very helpful.

The following organisations are a potential source of existing information:

SOURCE	TYPE OF INFORMATION
Ministry of Health	Health Information System: annual mortality rates, coverage of health services, in particular, measles immunisation. Availability of essential drugs, ORS, personnel. Nutrition: results of previous nutrition surveys, common causes of malnutrition, food habits. Organisations working in nutrition or undertaking surveys. Recommended survey methods/emergency procedures. Treatment guidelines. Training capacity.
Ministry of Agriculture	Statistics: population, livestock and harvests. Farming systems, markets and trading.
The department responsible for early warning.	Population statistics, changes in climate, farming systems, harvest projections, livestock holdings, coping mechanisms, markets. Contingency plans. Logistics.
The relief coordinating body	Current relief programmes: food-aid flows, logistics, major problems or constraints.
Other organisations	Their views of the situation. Logistics. Major problems or constraints.

2.2.2 Rapid assessments

Rapid assessment methods may be used to **gather new information quickly** during field visits. The purpose of a rapid assessment is to grasp the main points of the situation (how severe it is, the causes and who is most affected) quickly, without undertaking a full survey.

In assessments of food scarcity and famine these methods are rapid because fewer sites are visited than if a formal nutrition survey was undertaken.

Choose the sites for field visits carefully. They may be areas historically known to be the most affected by drought, or where destitute people are reportedly arriving and settling. Choose a variety of locations to allow comparison to be made.

Rapid assessments are largely based on **qualitative** information – views and opinions of the people you meet, and **personal observation** of conditions. Cross-checking your findings is essential because of the risk of misinformation. Use a range of rapid assessment methods to gather information from several sources in order to cross-check your findings.

The **advantages** of rapid assessments are:

● You 'learn as you go' rather than waiting to return to process your data.

● You find out about what local people think – a 'bottom-up approach'.

● Because they are quick, they save time and money.

● They often give unexpected information.

● They encourage the involvement of the community, who influence what you assess.

● They are less intrusive than formal interviews using questionnaires.

● There is no need for accurate population estimates.

The **disadvantages** of rapid assessments are:

● Bias may creep into your results undetected and so give you a false picture of the situation.

● The results only apply to the communities visited.

● It is difficult for people outside the team to verify the results, because statistical methods are not used.

● Direct observation limits you to what you see before you – there may be things you are not seeing.

Procedure for rapid assessments

Some of the different methods of gathering information during a rapid assessment are:

- **Semi-structured interviews**: informal interviews with people in the community.

- **Direct observation**: observing what is happening as a means of cross-checking findings or gathering new information.

- **Portraits and stories**: studying individuals or families and finding out personal histories.

- **Diagrams**: using drawings rather than words to record information (maps, seasonal calendars, history of events).

- **Ranking**: using exercises such as wealth ranking to learn more about certain aspects of the community.

Although they are described individually, rapid assessment techniques are used in **combination**. Although designed to provide information quickly, rapid assessment techniques are neither simple nor quick to learn and to use well. **Training and thorough preparation are essential**. (See Further Reading for some training manuals.)

There are several skills needed for rapid assessment. An ability to learn as you go is essential. Getting on with people from a variety of backgrounds is important. Experience of working with rural communities is a good basis for this work. **Interviewing skills** are vital. If experience is lacking, training is essential. It takes time to learn how to look, listen and encourage others to speak.

Rapid assessment is a **team effort**, all members work together, contributing their skills, knowledge and understanding. A team leader is important to bring together the work of each team member and to give direction. Field workers should be prepared to stay away from home and should not mind simple living conditions. (See also Section 2.3.2: The team.)

We will now look at the individual methods in more detail.

Semi-structured interviews

Semi-structured interviewing is a way of informally guiding a discussion to obtain information. The interviewer has a checklist of key areas they wish to learn about. The structure is flexible, to allow the interviewer to follow up points of interest ('probe') and ask new questions that arise as the discussion continues.

The skill of semi-structured interviewing is being able to **listen carefully**, to learn from what is said and to ask new questions to build on what is already known.

Interviews may be with **groups** or **individuals**. For example, groups might include village committees (local leaders, Red Cross/Crescent), or particular social groups (farmers, nomads). This is often more useful than talking with a random cross-section of the community, as within such a group several different views may be represented but not all will be heard. Within any social group, make sure that women and men are equally represented. Because of their different roles and situations, women and men may give different information, and it is therefore important to have both represented fully, to give a comprehensive picture. It may be difficult to talk with women in some communities, and they often speak more freely in the absence of men and in the company of other women. Within groups of women, older women may be dominant, or younger women be more confident because they have had some formal education.

Individuals of interest are either people who have a special knowledge – **key informants** – or ordinary people chosen as they are typical of a certain group in the community – **purposive sampling**. Examples of key informants include local chiefs or elders, government representatives, health workers, head of farmers' cooperative, leader of local women's group or local storytellers.

The more 'official' views of key informants are only one perspective of the situation and may differ from what other people think. It is easy to assume that people of authority are speaking on behalf of everybody. Check how true this is by talking to others.

The most important people to seek out are **those who are most vulnerable to food scarcity and famine** and are likely to be the poorest and closest to destitution. Women-headed households are likely to be one of the poorest groups in any community. Perceptions of who these people are will vary and it may not be in the interests of the key informants for you to identify them. To find the poorest people, visit the outskirts of the village where any recent migrants or the destitute might be living. Find out what the low-status jobs are and interview people doing them. Visit the local market and talk with casual traders, like people selling firewood or grass for fodder that they have collected themselves. **Get into the habit of finding people for yourself and do not always rely on the key informants taking you to them.**

People tend to be more on their guard during interviews, so talk to people in less formal settings, such as in tea or coffee houses, or at meals. Special efforts may be needed to find opportunities of listening to and talking with women.

(A training exercise to teach interviewing skills is described on page 36, and an example of a reporting form is shown on page 37.)

Direct observation

Direct observation is **learning by looking** and is one of the best ways to cross-check what people are telling you. For example, if stories of failed harvest and severe malnutrition are heard everywhere, have you seen them and if not why not? This may mean extra travelling and your hosts may feel offended and try to discourage you, but the object is to learn as much as you can about the whole situation.

If you see more than two or three extremely thin children in any single community, who seem subdued or miserable or have visibly protruding bones and loose skin, there is likely to be a serious nutrition problem. Severely malnourished children are obvious even to a layperson, but if there are only one or two, the malnutrition may be due to very poor individual circumstances and not a result of a more general decline. Moderately malnourished children are much more difficult to spot by eye.

Take advantage of household visits to look around you. Wealth or poverty are rarely obvious, so interpret what you see with caution.

Important sites that it may be worth visiting in each location include the market place, the health centre, the baker or mill and the water source.

Portraits and stories

Portraits and stories are a way of bringing to life the reality of people's lives – their actual living conditions and the problems facing them. They are a good way of describing how food scarcity and famine are affecting particular groups of people and how they are coping.

Diagrams

Presenting information in the form of diagrams makes it clear and easy to understand. A lot of descriptive information may be summarised in a single diagram. Drawing diagrams is a way of thinking through and understanding your information. Written text can sometimes conceal muddled thinking, whereas it is obvious if diagrams are unclear.

Diagrams are useful as the **focus for a discussion**. For example, during an interview you could draw a diagram on a large sheet of paper or on the ground to show what you have learnt from the discussion. People can then discuss with you the gaps in your understanding.

Examples of useful diagrams are maps, historic profiles and seasonal calenders. Historic profiles show the nature and relative severity of recent events. Seasonal calenders summarise all the changes that occur throughout the year, including times of difficulty or stress. An example of a detailed seasonal calender is shown in Figure 4.

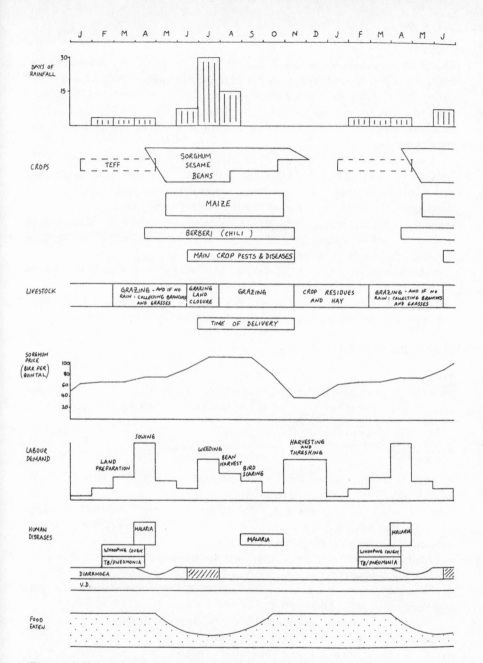

Figure 4: Example of a seasonal calender

Extract from *An Introduction to Rapid Rural Appraisal for Agricultural Development*, McCracken, J.A., Pretty, J.N. and Conway, G.R., London, I.I.E.D.

Ranking

Ranking exercises are a way of finding out people's perceptions of the order of importance of things. For example, you could ask people to rank **problems**: *'What is the most serious problem facing you at the moment?'*. Then go on to ask about the next most serious problem. Such questions must always be followed up (probed) by asking: *'Why, and what will you be able to do about it?'* Or questions might be about the future: *'In six months' time or after the harvest, what problems will you face?'*

Ranking could be used to construct a **seasonal calender**. You ask people: *'Which month do you have most food to eat?'* and continue until you have an idea of seasonal availability of food. Labour patterns can be drawn up by asking people: *'Which month do you have the most work to do?'*, followed by questions about the type of work. As the person is talking to you, draw a diagram showing the distribution of labour over the year to see if you have understood correctly.

Wealth ranking is a way of learning about and understanding people's perceptions of the differences in wealth between households in the community. Applied with care, it can give a lot of relevant information quickly. Wealth ranking can provide useful information that complements nutrition status data. Recently, Oxfam has used wealth ranking as part of nutrition surveys. The families of those children who were found to be malnourished in nutrition surveys were ranked by people in the community according to their wealth. The wealth ranking method is described in Appendix 2.

2.2.3 Nutrition surveys

Surveys provide **quantitative** information about the population. For example, a nutrition survey estimates the rate or prevalence of malnutrition in the population. Other quantitative household information may also be collected during a nutrition survey.

Anthropometric (body) measurements of children are used to estimate the rate of malnutrition (see page 27, and also Appendix 5 which explains how to measure children). The prevalence of malnutrition among children in a whole population is estimated from the results of measuring a sample of children. The accuracy of these statistical estimates depends on **correct sampling methods** and careful measurements.

The prevalence of malnutrition in the sample is expressed as a single figure, known as the **point prevalence**; for example, 14.3 per cent of the children in the sample are malnourished. This refers only to the sample, and not to the whole population from which the sample was taken. The results from the sample can then be used to estimate the prevalence of malnutrition in the whole population. This estimate is expressed as a range of values known as

confidence limits (rather than a single figure like the point prevalence). For example, the rate of malnutrition in the population might be estimated to be between 12.3 and 21.0 per cent. The confidence limits are 12.3 and 21.0 and the **confidence interval** is 8.7. (Methods for selecting a sample for a nutrition survey are explained in Appendix 3 and survey statistics in Appendix 4.)

Because the rates of malnutrition for a population are estimates, based on samples, there is a chance that they may be inaccurate, that is, that the true rate of malnutrition in the population lies outside the confidence limits. We can express this in terms of probability. A 95 per cent confidence interval means that it is 95 per cent certain that the rate for the population is within the confidence limits, but that there is a 5 per cent, or one in twenty, chance that the estimate is incorrect.

You can link quantitative and qualitative data by using the results of the initial assessment and the rapid assessment to interpret the meaning of the quantitative data from a formal survey (see Section 2.4: Analysing and interpreting your findings).

Planning and carrying out a formal survey requires knowledge and experience of survey design, sampling and statistics. Measuring children requires literacy, numeracy and accuracy (see Appendix 5: Measuring children). Experience of rural field conditions is also important, otherwise your proposed sampling methods may be impossible to apply in practice. **If you do not have these skills, think seriously before you start a survey because wrong information is even worse than no information**!

The **advantages** of formal surveys are that:

- They can be used to measure changes in the nutritional status of a population over time.

- They allow comparisons to be made between different groups in the survey or with the results of other surveys which used similar methods.

- The accuracy of results may be verified by checking the methods and statistics that were used.

- Several different locations are visited, and team members have direct contact with people in their own homes.

- Objective measures of malnutrition are useful for monitoring the impact of a relief programme.

The **disadvantages** of formal surveys are that:

- They may take several weeks to complete.

- Considerable resources are needed (personnel, vehicles, fuel) to carry them out.

- Field workers may be withdrawn from other vital work in order to carry out a survey.

- Measuring children can be intrusive and inconvenient. Non-cooperation may be a problem and could lead to unreliable results.

- Surveys are often planned and results analysed far from the survey sites, with little or no involvement of people from the community.

- Working from an inflexible questionnaire hinders a relaxed discussion with the person being interviewed.

- The overall rate of malnutrition for the population may not be disaggregated for smaller groups within the population, so that differential rates of malnutrition of groups within the surveyed population will not be shown up.

Procedure for carrying out surveys

You first need to make some decisions about what to measure and whom to measure. Nutrition indices are body measurements related to age or height, and are used to estimate malnutrition by comparing the individuals with the healthy reference population (see Section 1.2 Nutrition and malnutrition).

An inadequate diet and/or infection may lead to weight loss. In the short term, a child suffering weight loss becomes thin or **wasted**. This is known as **acute malnutrition**, and is reflected by the nutrition indices **weight for height or length** (WFH/L) and **mid-upper arm circumference** (MUAC).

Thinness can develop very rapidly and may occur seasonally, during the 'hungry season' which is often just before the harvest. The prevalence of thinness is greatest between 12 and 24 months of age, which is when infants are often weaned. During this time dietary deficiencies are common and diarrhoeal diseases frequent. Under favourable conditions weight can be restored rapidly.

A poor diet over a longer period may cause growth failure so the child may be short for their age or **stunted.** This is reflected by the **height for age** (HFA) index. Unlike weight loss, growth failure is not necessarily reversible.

Weight for height or length (WFH/L)

Weight for height is the most common nutrition index used in nutrition surveys. An individual's height and weight are compared with those of the reference population by calculating percentage weight for height or length (% WFH/L). This is the child's weight expressed as a percentage of the average weight of children of the same height. The method of calculating weight for height or length is given in Appendix 4: Survey Statistics.

An individual child's weight and height measurements may also be expressed as **'Z scores'**. Z scores express a child's weight as a multiple of the standard deviation (a measure of the spread of values around the mean) of the reference population, and are also known as 'standard deviation scores'. They are statistically more correct than percentages of the reference median WFH, but are a little more complicated to calculate and less easy to understand. A full explanation of Z scores, and the method of calculating them, are given in Appendix 4: Survey Statistics.

Mid upper arm circumference (MUAC)

Measuring MUAC is quicker than measuring both weight and height and then calculating the percentage WFH/L or Z score. Consequently, MUAC is frequently used to screen large numbers of children in search of those who may be malnourished (see Section 4.3 Supplementary Feeding).

MUAC may seem easier to measure than WFH, but experienced field workers have expressed concern that it is easy to make mistakes when measuring arm circumference, either by pulling the tape too tight or by leaving it loose, especially if the child is anxious and their arm is not relaxed. Despite these problems, MUAC is as good or even better than WFH/L for the identification of malnourished children. If you decide to use it, make every effort to ensure measurements are made correctly (see Appendix 5: How to measure children).

The same terms are used to classify malnutrition however it is measured. Children are described as adequately nourished, moderately malnourished or severely malnourished. Table 3 gives the cut-off points for defining levels of malnutrition for the different indices we have described.

| | Weight for height/length | | MUAC |
	%WFH/L	Z score	cm
Adequately nourished	>79.9	> -1.9	>13.4
Moderately malnourished	<80 and >69.9	< -2 and > -2.9	<13.5 and >12.4
Severely malnourished	<70	< -3.0	<12.5

Table 3: Classification of nutritional status

The results of MUAC and WFH/L surveys are not comparable. When they are both measured on the same children, MUAC tends to give larger estimates of the percentage of children who are malnourished. It is not possible to predict from a MUAC survey the level of malnutrition that would be shown by a WFH/L survey.

This means that you should **always use the nutritional index that has been used for previous surveys in the area** where you are working. If in doubt consult the local Ministry of Health and previous survey reports.

Measuring adults

There are large variations in the height and body composition of adults throughout the world and therefore it is harder to interpret the body measurements of adults in terms of nutritional status.

The body mass index (BMI) is used in industrialised countries to establish levels of risk. BMI is a numerical index which does not itself relate to any reference population.

$$BMI = \text{Weight in kg} / (\text{Height in m})^2$$

Because there is little information about risks attached to low levels of BMI, it is only useful for monitoring purposes. The following cut-off points are being considered by WHO:

BMI above 18: Adequate nutrition

BMI below 16: Evidence for chronic energy deficiency

Sampling

Having decided what to measure, you now have to decide who to measure. It is rarely possible to include everybody in the population in a survey, so to save time and money a limited number of people are chosen. The choice of people is known as **sampling** and the people chosen are the **sample**.

The characteristics of the sample should be similar to the characteristics of the total population. This is what is meant by '**a representative sample**'. A sample that does not represent the population is said to be **biased**. For example, if mothers volunteer to have their children measured, rather than being randomly selected, this would result in a biased sample.

When the total population is included in the survey, for example, when all the children in a community are measured, it is known as a **census**, and is no longer a sample survey. The results of a census only apply to the population measured.

Simple random sampling

Simple random sampling is where every individual or household has an **equal chance of being chosen** for the sample. For example, picking names out of a hat, or at random from a list. Simple random sampling is appropriate where lists of all individuals or households are available and the people chosen are easy to find.

Interval sampling

In this system of sampling, people are selected from the population at **equal intervals**, for example, every fiftieth person on a list. The first person is selected by choosing a number at random between 1 and 50, using random number tables. If this number is 31, the next will be 81 (31+50), followed by 131 (81+50) and so on.

Cluster sampling

In cluster sampling, instead of selecting people individually, as with the previous sampling methods, **groups of people** are chosen. Each group is known as a cluster. The results for all the individual clusters are combined to give an estimate for the whole population.

Most nutrition surveys use cluster sampling to select the children to be measured. It is easier to apply in practice than simple random sampling because it is not necessary to have a complete list of all children in the total population; and fewer places are visited, which saves time (the number visited corresponds to the number of clusters).

Samples for cluster surveys must be **double the size of an equivalent** simple random sample because estimates based on clusters are less accurate than ones obtained from sampling selected individuals. A cluster survey gives a single estimate of malnutrition, which is an average of all the clusters looked at and should not be divided further. The results from a few clusters should not be used to give estimates of malnutrition for a small area within the cluster survey, because they would not give a sufficiently accurate estimate.

Sample size for cluster surveys

The sample size in a cluster survey is equal to the number of clusters multiplied by the number of children measured in each cluster. Statisticians recommend **at least 24 clusters, and preferably 30 clusters**, for estimating the rate of malnutrition in a population. Less than 24 clusters are likely to give misleading results.

Cluster sampling can be used if you wish to look for differences between population groups or geographical areas. You will need to select 24 to 30 clusters to survey from each area or group of interest.

In a single camp or large village, cluster surveys may take only a few days and so it is possible to survey several different camps. It will be much more difficult to make comparisons between home-based populations living in different regions, as each survey in a single region may take two to three weeks due to the distances that must be travelled.

In each cluster between 10 and 30 children should be measured. Any more than 30 children will be time-consuming and allow little time for other activities such as interviewing. **It is better to have more clusters with fewer children in each than to have fewer clusters with more children in each.** The system for selecting clusters for a nutrition survey is explained in Appendix 3.

Unequal cluster sizes

In the past some surveys have measured all children present in a village rather than a fixed number of children. Sometimes it can be difficult to select children at random from a community. By measuring all children present your results will show the rate of malnutrition for that community. However, there are disadvantages in measuring all children present. If the number of children is large, it may take longer than one day to measure them all, leaving little time for meeting and talking with people. In any case, it is likely that some children will be absent, and this could bias your results.

Survey statistics based on unequal cluster sizes are more complicated to calculate and for that reason, are not included in Appendix 4: Survey Statistics. However, if you are doing a large survey which includes more than 24 clusters, the effects of unequal cluster size should be less and so the statistical methods in Appendix 4 may be used.

The area covered by a survey

The area which a survey should cover depends partly on the variation in rates of malnutrition which you expect to find within the area you wish to survey.

The cluster method assumes that the rate of malnutrition is similar throughout the area to be surveyed. This may be true in normal times, but in times of food scarcity, **pockets of malnutrition often develop within a region**. These pockets will not necessarily be detected by a cluster survey of the entire region as only the average rate of malnutrition for the region will be known.

It may therefore be more useful to make **separate surveys of individual villages**, which are chosen to represent different types of village, such as the most affected (from anecdotal evidence or local knowledge), the better off, those with important markets, those frequented by nomads, etc. Rates of malnutrition may then be estimated for each village, but it will not be statistically valid to use the figures obtained to make estimates for the area as a whole.

Before deciding to embark on a formal survey, you need to ask yourself whether or not a survey is practical in your situation.

Where people are home-based over a large geographical region, it is sometimes difficult to apply cluster survey methods correctly because of field constraints which make these methods impractical. You should consider whether any of the following constraints apply to your situation.

Common survey constraints and ways of overcoming them

PROBLEM: SOLUTION

Scattered population over a large area: Allow more time for travelling between sites and select a small number of children per cluster to ensure that the same number is found in each site.

Limited access to some areas because of insecurity or inadequate roads: If access is impossible, then a random sample of the area cannot be taken. The alternative is to select a sample of people who have recently left the area, for example, to attend a food distribution or health clinic, or on market day. This will give you a biased (unrepresentative) sample, and only a very rough indication of the true picture. If roads are inadequate, try alternative means of transport such as walking, mules or camels.

Limited time: This is often the greatest constraint. There are no short cuts to getting accurate estimates of malnutrition. The only alternative is to reduce the size of the area surveyed. For example, instead of undertaking a cluster survey of a large area, make a survey in each of several small villages. Either measure all children in each village or, if the villages are large, randomly select 24 to 30 clusters from each. Villages may be chosen randomly or it may be more useful to sample them purposively, for example:
 – the worst or least affected;
 – where destitute people are to be found;
 – those villages receiving food aid.

Variation in the rate of malnutrition is suspected: A cluster survey of the entire region will give you a single estimate of the rate of malnutrition and will not show differences within that region. Divide the area into smaller sections, according to where you think the differences are, and select between 24 and 30 clusters from each.

No reliable data on population size: Use as many sources of information as possible to list all known villages in the area to be surveyed. Estimate the relative size, based on local knowledge, and assign a relative score to each location (very big = 5, big = 4, medium = 3, small = 2 and very small = 1). Use these estimates of size to select the required number of villages randomly (see Appendix 3).

Cluster surveys of nomads: The whereabouts of nomads is hard to predict and so it is difficult to make a reliable list of all nomad camps to select clusters from. To include nomads in the survey you will have to be determined and allow extra time for travelling. Two options are to list sites where nomads are known to gather, such as watering points or markets and then to choose a number of these at random; or visit randomly selected villages and ask the whereabouts of the nearest nomadic group, then use these groups in your sample. Reduce the cluster size, as nomadic groups are often small and have few children.

Remember that inappropriate changes to survey methods are liable to give misleading results.

2.3 Planning your assessment and organising your team

2.3.1 Time scales

The time taken to complete your assessment depends on what you hope to achieve. The time involved for carrying out the different stages of your assessment should be estimated:

Initial assessments: Up to one week.

Organising the field trip: Up to one week.

Rapid field assessments: Minimum of half to one day in each community, plus travelling time between communities.

Nutrition survey field work: If people are in a small area (a camp or large village) – 2 to 3 days. If people are dispersed over a large area – 2 to 3 weeks minimum, more likely to be 4 to 6 weeks (based on 30 clusters and one survey team).

Analyses and report writing: One to two weeks.

Write out a timetable of activities to plan realistic deadlines. Where food and accommodation is basic and the team is working long days, limit field trips to one week. Trips of two to three weeks without a break or return home are exhausting and the quality of the work will suffer.

2.3.2 The team

It is important to have an experienced **team leader**, who has helped in planning the assessment and will play an active part in carrying it out.

The number of **team members** depends on the work to be done and the transport available. A Landrover or Landcruiser holds six people, their luggage and extra fuel, but will then be very full. It is better to have a team of five and keep an extra space for picking up local guides, translators or volunteers.

The gender balance of the team is important; the team must always include women, and they must be seen to have authority within the team. In almost every situation, individual women or groups of women will talk more readily and openly to women interviewers than to men. Interviewing is best done by **two people**; one to direct the interview, while the other listens, takes notes and prompts if necessary. Weighing and measuring of children requires **three people**; two to measure and one to record information. The most experienced person should read the actual measurements and take responsibility for checking that children are positioned properly.

The **driver** is a key member of the team and will often contribute far more than just their driving skills, for example, knowledge about road conditions and access problems. He or she will also be able to talk informally with other drivers who are often well-informed about unusual happenings. Maintaining a vehicle on the road is a major task and so the driver should not be expected to also double as a translator or weigh children (although they will probably help occasionally).

Involve people from the local community as much as possible. Consider whether some payment to cover the living costs of local volunteers is appropriate.

Other important points to remember are that an expatriate in the team may raise expectations among local people, who might see the team as belonging to a 'wealthy' foreign organisation. An expatriate may also require someone to act as translator.

A more experienced team may be had by 'borrowing' staff from government ministries and other organisations. In this way, you are more likely to find experienced and knowledgeable field workers. The involvement of more than one reputable organisation will also give the results greater credibility.

2.3.3 Training

The team should understand the **purpose** of the assessment and the **principles** of the methods used.

Weighing and measuring techniques are described in Appendix 5. Team members should be well-practised before the survey. A visit to a local PHC clinic where growth monitoring is undertaken would be useful training.

During a rapid assessment, the interviewers are continually learning and using their new knowledge to form new questions. This active learning role is demanding and very different from completing structured questionnaires. Switching from formal questionnaires to semi-structured interviewing requires training and practical experience to develop the necessary skills. A training exercise will allow the team to plan together to decide who the team should see and what information they hope to find out, and also teach the principles of the methods used.

Other topics to discuss with the team during training are interview techniques and recording forms.

Interview techniques

- Start with the **appropriate greetings** and wait until people are sitting comfortably and are ready for you to introduce yourselves. Expatriates are often regarded as rude and impatient when they launch into a speech before proper introductions are made.

- Explain the **purpose of your visit** and give a brief summary of what you would like to talk about. Be frank, honest and absolutely clear about your intentions. You have come to learn about what is happening. Raising expectations does irreparable damage to relations with people and may bias information you are given.

- Leave any difficult questions until mid-way through the interview and try to close on a subject pleasing to the group or person.

- Individual interviews should take less than one hour and group interviews no longer than two hours or everyone will get tired.

Interviewing problems

Be aware of how **bias** will creep in. For example, by paying more attention to the views of the educated and articulate, or focusing on information or ideas that will confirm your views. Beware of favouring the ideas of those who agree with you.

Role playing during training exercises may reveal unhelpful attitudes of the assessors towards certain groups in the community, for example, towards women or people belonging to certain social groups.

The way you phrase your questions will influence and even bias the response. Questions that can be answered by yes or no, (*'Have you any livestock?'*) are not very useful. Remember the six helpful words – **who, where, when, how, why and what** – and try to begin all your questions with one of these words. Avoid 'leading questions', which suggest the answer. For example, *'should not something be done about ....'*.

Other common interviewing faults include: failure to listen; interrupting; failure to probe (to follow-up unclear or unexpected answers by requests for clarification); lack of attention to detail; uncritical acceptance of answers. During group interviews, try not to allow one or two people to dominate the discussions.

A training exercise

1. Discuss with the team the key areas of information you want to know about. Use the questions and sources of information listed in Table 2 to guide your discussion.

2. List the main areas of interest on a large sheet of paper.

3. Next to each area list the people you might interview about these areas. Remember to include several different sources for each area of interest.

4. Ask the team members to make up questions about these areas using any of the six ways of starting a question – who, where, when, how, why and what. Forming questions forces the team to think about how they will approach difficult or sensitive topics. (During the actual interview, only the checklist of areas of interest is used, as written questions make the interview less flexible.)

5. Use these questions in role-playing exercises, in which members of the team take turns to pretend to be local people and are interviewed by the others. (You will need to prepare, in advance of the training exercise, notes on the characteristics of the people to be interviewed, to give to the person playing that role.)

6. After the role playing, discuss the questions asked. Was there enough attention to detail or were the interviewers content just to have an answer? Did the interviewers accept everything they were told or did they probe to see how reliable a particular answer was?

7. Point out what was good about the team's interviewing skills, and what needs improvement.

2.3.4 Recording information

Forms are needed to record both **qualitative** and **quantitative** information. They should be designed in advance and tested in the practice interviews.

Most of the data from rapid assessments is either descriptive or qualitative (views and opinions). A simple notebook for each member of the team should suffice for recording most of their observations and the results from interviews. Each entry should include date, location, details of informant and general subject area. Make notes under each of the checklist headings. Include observations, hunches or ideas and any doubts about the reliability of the information recorded.

If possible, record the results from semi-structured interviews after the interview has taken place. This makes it easier for the interviewer to concentrate on what is being said during the interview and to follow up important points. The interview will be more like a normal discussion and less intimidating for the person being interviewed. However, learning to listen and remember is a skill that takes time to develop. If notes are taken during an interview, try and arrange for people to work in teams of at least two, so one person can direct the discussion while the other takes notes.

The use of forms tends to introduce a rigid structure to the talk that puts the respondent in a passive role of answering questions rather than actively taking part in a discussion.

Survey forms

Well-designed reporting forms are vital for collecting quantitative information in surveys. In nutrition surveys the most valuable quantitative information is **anthropometric data** and **population figures**. Household size and structure may also be useful in planning ration sizes. However, remember that there is always a temptation to add more questions than are really necessary.

An example of an appropriate anthropometric reporting form is shown in Figure 5. Instead of recording each child's results on a single questionnaire, the results of up to 30 children are recorded on a single page; the results for each child are recorded on a single line of the form. This greatly reduces the number of forms needed. There are columns on the form for the calculation of each child's percentage weight for height or length, and for categorising the child's nutritional status. This column format allows the results to be quickly summarised in the field.

ANTHROPOMETRIC DATA REPORTING FORM

SURVEY LOCATION : Region _____ Village _____ Sheet number ____

Date _____ Team Leader_____ Cluster number _____

Child number	Sex M - male F -female	Age Months	Arm circum- ference Cm	Weight Kg	Height or length cm	Percent weight for height %	Classification <70%	70%- <80%	>80%	Remarks

Figure 5: A form to record anthropometric data from a nutritional survey

Recording protein energy malnutrition

As well as recording weights and heights or lengths, you should record any of the characteristic signs of protein energy malnutrition (PEM). Protein energy malnutrition is a range of clinical disorders; the two extremes are **marasmus** and **kwashiorkor**, between which are less well defined forms which show a mixture of the features of marasmus and kwashiorkor:

Marasmus: loose folds of skin around the thighs and buttocks ('baggy pants'); sunken eyes; little or no fat; and muscles flabby rather than firm and strong (wasting).

Kwashiorkor: swelling around the ankles and sometimes in the upper arms and face (oedema) – the child may even appear fat. To check for oedema, press the area on the back of the foot or shin and see if a dent remains after you remove your finger. Hair changes (light in colour, brittle, pulls out easily); skin changes (flaky, raw and weeping areas); children are miserable, apathetic and have no appetite.

Marasmic kwashiorkor: A combination of the signs of marasmus and kwashiorkor. The child is thin and wasted, with swollen lower limbs.

Other information

When children are measured, it is difficult to ask mothers any more than the most simple questions and it is not a good time to discuss sensitive issues. If additional household information or discussion is needed, arrange separate household interviews and use another reporting form.

Individual household questionnaires are only needed for in-depth household interviews designed to obtain detailed quantitative information. For quick nutritional surveys it may be a waste of time to collect a lot of quantitative household information, such as information about food stores, assets or livestock. It is difficult to get precise answers and it is hard to judge how reliable any answers are. Also, nobody likes being asked detailed personal questions and this reluctance may hinder a more general discussion about the situation.

It may be more worthwhile concentrating on more qualitative but in-depth information by using rapid assessment methods, in particular, semi-structured interviewing.

Where only a few questions are being asked of each household, a recording form similar to the anthropometric reporting form in Figure 5 should suffice. Each household corresponds to a single line and their answers to each question are recorded in adjacent columns. The questions are written on a separate sheet. During the actual interview it is preferable if the interviewer can memorise the questions and simply use the recording form as a prompt.

A **pilot assessment** of a nearby community is useful practice for the team. Pre-testing of recording forms should reveal any problems which can then be put right before starting the actual assessment.

2.3.5 Resources needed for nutrition surveys

We list below what Oxfam nutrition survey teams in Sudan commonly take with them on field trips, which should cover most needs:

Transport:
Roadworthy vehicle(s).
Enough fuel in jerry cans.
Spares: 2 spare wheels, accelerator cable, fan belt, jack, tyre, pump, tow rope.
Water for cooling engine (hot conditions).
First aid kit.
Tools.

Survey equipment
Height and length board
(see Appendix 5: construction of a height/length board).
2 x 25kg spring balance Salter scales with bar for larger children (1 spare).
10 or 12kg weight to check balance.
Hanging pants/ basket for infants.
Arm circumference strips.
Clip boards.
Notebooks.
Recording forms.
Pens, pencils, rubbers, rulers.
Calculators.

Food and bedding
Sleeping mats, blankets or sleeping bags for the whole team.
Food supplies in case food unavailable locally.
Cooking fuel and equipment.
Drinking and washing water.

Miscellaneous
Money – payment for food, accommodation, repaying hospitality, or to cover expenses of volunteers.
Travel permits and papers.
Letters of introduction.

Communications

Before leaving on a field trip, develop a system for communicating with your office and inform them of your timetable and expected date of return. Inform the relevant departments in the government, UN, or other organisations, of your plans.

Situations of insecurity

Working in situations of food scarcity and famine have been hampered in the past by problems of insecurity due to armed conflict. You should constantly assess the risks of travelling your proposed route. Ask the opinions of people who are well informed and familiar with the area as to the degree of danger.

2.4 Analysing and interpreting your findings

Do not wait until you have completed your fieldwork before beginning to analyse and understand your findings. During fieldwork you 'learn as you go'. Record important points in a notebook as soon as you can. Include observations, ideas or hunches. Remember to record the reasons behind them. Label notes with the date, location and name(s) of relevant people.

The team should regularly discuss their findings together. This may bring out important points or indicate necessary changes in the assessment methods.

If possible, before leaving each location, calculate the percentage weight for height or Z score for each child and classify their nutritional status. Also calculate the proportion malnourished in the sample (see Appendix 4).

Discuss your findings with the community leaders and note their reactions:

- Are the findings important to them?

- Are they concerned about the malnourished or destitute or do they have other priorities?

- What is their analysis of the situation?

2.4.1 Analysing nutrition status results

On completion of field work, it can be a daunting task to make sense of a mass of reporting forms and notes. The statistical analysis of nutrition data from formal surveys is explained in Appendix 4. There is a range of statistical information you might aim to produce, including :

- The **proportion** of children malnourished in the sample.

- The **standard error** of the proportion malnourished.

- The **confidence interval** for the proportion malnourished in the population.

- The **average nutrition status** of the children in the sample.

- The **standard error** of the mean.

- The **confidence interval** for the mean in the population.

Worked through examples are shown in Appendix 4, which use a set of nutrition data from a cluster survey of two large villages in Sudan. The data are the percentage weight for height measurements of 300 children.

Computer software

Micro-computer software* is now available for computing anthropometric data, specifically height for age, weight for age and weight for age indices based on the CDC/WHO international reference population. It takes time to learn how to use these programmes and, unless you already have the necessary skills, in an emergency situation it is probably quicker to make manual calculations.

Presenting survey data

Try to keep your analyses simple. Diagrams can be a useful way of presenting ideas. You may find it helpful to summarise the main points in a table. Results should fall naturally under a number of headings and these should be the same as the main points on your original checklist of information needs.

An example of a table showing the results from a nutrition survey:

	WEIGHT FOR HEIGHT			
	Below 70% WFH	70% - below 80% WFH	80% WFH & over	Average % WFH
Number of children	4	61	235	85·2%
Proportion	1·3%	20·3%	78·7%	
Confidence limits	0·1%-2·5%	15·4%-25·2%		

Figure 6: Summary of the results of the nutrition survey in Gorem District

* For information about Anthro, CASP, Epi Info contact:
Nutrition Unit, World Health Organisation, 1211 Geneva 27, Switzerland
(Epi Info and CASP may be used for generalised data entry and Anthro may be of use for batch processing of data that has already been typed into a spreadsheet or data base.)

Do not present data that represents a single cluster unless the cluster represents all children in a particular location. If it does, then the results are representative of that community on that day. In this case present in your table:

- The **number** of children measured.

- The **proportion** moderately and severely malnourished.

- The **average nutritional status** of children in the community.

When your analysis of the data is complete, hold a meeting for team members to discuss the findings. Pin the tables and diagrams on a wall for all to see.

2.4.2 Interpreting nutritional status results

In isolation, rates of malnutrition only tell part of the story. To understand the process that has led to malnutrition you need to consider the wider situation and to look for the **underlying causes** of malnutrition (see Section 2.1.2).

Remember that data can be misleading. For example, a survey after an outbreak of measles or at the end of the hungry season will show levels of malnutrition that are cause for concern, yet the children are likely to recover quickly and the high incidence of malnutrition does not mean that famine is imminent. On the other hand, even in times of extreme food scarcity, the rate of malnutrition may not appear abnormal. This may be because mothers keep the most nourishing food for their youngest children. **Too much reliance on statistics can be dangerous**: when rates of malnutrition do not change over time, this may mask a deteriorating situation, in which the most severely malnourished children are dying and are replaced in the statistics by others who have recently become malnourished.

In order to interpret nutrition status results correctly, you should consider how your results compare with data from previous surveys or other surveys in the same area. **Only make comparisons where similar survey methods have been used**. Try to determine the underlying causes of the malnutrition you have observed; is malnutrition a chronic problem in the area, or has it recently worsened? Is it likely to get worse or better and why? Which groups seem to be worst affected and why? Be alert for possible gender differences in nutritional status.

It is also important to **review local attitudes to malnutrition**; is it thought to be a health problem and if so, what are people doing about it? Are the local health services aware of the problem and if so what are they doing about it; for example, what is the coverage of measles immunisation?

Thin children are just one sign of a general deterioration in the situation and there may be other **potentially more serious problems**, for example, the erosion of people's livelihoods to a point where they are destitute and must leave their homes in search of food. In this situation it is more important to support the whole family while they are still in the relative safety oftheir own home. **Once families migrate, the risks to their health are likely to escalate**.

Malnutrition is important, but **beware of making it the priority problem to be tackled when there are other, more pressing issues**.

The need for supplementary feeding programmes

Rates of malnutrition should not generally be used to trigger a response such as supplementary feeding automatically, because the health risks associated with particular rates of malnutrition vary in every situation.

Health risks tend to be much greater in camps of displaced people than among home based populations. For example, in a camp of 40,000 displaced people a rate of malnutrition of 15 per cent may require immediate action in terms of selective feeding, whereas the same rate among drought affected village communities may be of much less concern, especially if immunisation coverage is high and access to water and sanitation are good.

In *Selective Feeding Programmes (Oxfam Practical Health Guide 1)* a rate of malnutrition of 20 per cent is suggested as a rough guide to the need for selective feeding in a refugee camp. However, in practice, the decision to start selective feeding is based on several other factors, such as availability of resources and access to the programme.

2.5 Presenting your findings

Informing the communities concerned

Before you leave a village, discuss with local leaders the preliminary findings of the assessment, and comment on their situation in relation to neighbouring villages. Explain clearly that you can make no promises and that this visit is just the first stage of learning about them and providing an opportunity for them to meet agency staff.

Describe to them the next stages of your work; visiting other villages, returning to the regional centre to make a report, discussing your findings with your superiors and other organisations and looking into the feasibility of any proposals.

If possible, on your return to headquarters send a letter of thanks and maybe a summary report to one of your contacts in the village.

Report writing

Plan the layout of your report before you start to write. (The most common format is shown in Appendix 6.) Include a contents list at the beginning of your report. Keep the report as short as possible and include only relevant information, avoiding duplication. A table, graph, diagram or map can save pages of text and be easier to understand.

Use headings to break up the text and act as signposts pointing out what is to be found in each section. Use a decimal system for numbering your headings (1., 1.1., 1.2., 1.3, 2., 2.1 etc.).

Your writing style should be simple, clear and concise, with short, simple and active sentence structures. Use familiar words; choose the simpler of two words that have the same meaning e.g. 'begin' instead of 'initiate'. Do not use ambiguous or needless words and avoid jargon. It is often better to use a personal pronoun than make writing impersonal. Impersonal writing can be cumbersome and ambiguous.

A word processor speeds up writing reports and makes editing much easier. **Concentrate on improving the quality and style of your writing rather than increasing the quantity.**

Oral briefings

Be prepared to talk to people about the key points raised in your assessment. Many people do not have time to read reports.

You may need to present your findings at a large meeting. Prepare your briefing beforehand and base it on the summary of the report. In longer presentations tables, diagrams or maps are helpful. Be informative and present **factual information**. Be clear as to the recommendations arising from your assessment.

A workshop or seminar may be an appropriate way of sharing information more widely. Results may then be discussed with others before decisions are taken. Work out a timetable that includes relevant presentations, time for discussion and for summarising the outcome of the discussion.

Telephone, radio and telex messages

Messages by phone, telex and radio are often the first briefing your office receives and should be simple, clear and concise. Messages expressing concern about a situation will be acted upon, so it is vital that your message is correct.

Number all messages sequentially and keep a file of them in order. Break up the text into short numbered sections. Use short sentences and familiar words.

If the telex is to **inform**, first summarise the main points:

● Date of assessment.

● Names of affected areas, names of villages visited.

● Details of affected population; estimated numbers, ethnic group, composition, home-based or destitute, other available relevant statistics (rate of malnutrition, number of deaths).

- Response of government and other organisations.

- Details of reports to follow.

Then state in more detail the main conclusions: the causes of the problem; future trends; possible role for the agency.

If the telex is recommending **action**, first state the recommended action, then give the main reasons for this recommendation and a statement of costs, resources needed, timings and more detailed justification.

PART THREE:

USING YOUR FINDINGS IN MAKING DECISIONS

Before making your assessment you will have considered the decisions that have to be made, as discussed in Part 2, Section 1. The three key decision-making areas are:

● **The appropriate response.**

● **Targeting.**

● **Your agency's role.**

How these decisions are linked with the findings of your assessment and your analyses of the situation are considered in this part of the manual. Section 3.1 reviews the points which must be considered in your analysis of the situation when deciding the response or actions needed. In Section 3.2, different interventions are considered in relation to the main objectives underlying any response to a situation of food scarcity and famine. Section 3.3 describes the concept of targeting and whether it may be appropriate. This depends on being able to identify which groups are the priority (who is most affected) and the administrative constraints of trying to target these groups.

3.1 Your analysis of the situation

The severity of the problem

It is important to distinguish between the immediate life-threatening nature of famine and the less immediate but nevertheless severe effects of food scarcity. Famine is much more visible than food scarcity – people may be hungry, malnourished, ill or even dying. These obvious signs of distress are much more measurable than the insidious effects of food scarcity. It is very difficult to measure the damage to people's livelihoods caused by food scarcity or the distress that results. To outsiders nothing much may seem to be happening.

The causes of the problem

Consider whether food availability or people's entitlements to that food are more important causal factors. This should influence which type of response might be appropriate and who it should be directed towards. For example, providing cash for work programmes may be inappropriate where food cannot be readily purchased.

The people at risk

Situations of food scarcity affect people differently. Some people may even benefit as a result of food scarcity; for example, increases in the price of basic foods may benefit small farmers who have produce to sell, while severely affecting those people who must buy their food from the market (labourers, pastoralists). Some individuals may prosper and become rich, for example, those who are able to buy livestock at low prices and move them to areas of pasture and water elsewhere.

Identifying those areas and people who are most vulnerable to the effects of food scarcity and famine is the first stage of **targeting.** This will be dealt with fully in Section 3.3.

The role of government and non-governmental agencies

Many African countries have achieved remarkable success in substantially reducing the threat of famine. It is important to recognise the role and responsibilities of government and local institutions in responding to food scarcity and famine. In the long term it is the commitment and policies of governments that will be the driving force that eradicates famines, rather than the temporary efforts of relief agencies.

International agencies may be in a strong position to support and complement the government relief programme. In particular, the knowledge, experience, and additional resources of agencies may be of assistance in identifying more appropriate interventions or even gaps in the relief programme, such as the unidentified needs of particular groups of people.

Administrative and logistical problems are the main reasons why most relief programmes fail to meet their objectives. Long delays in delivering food assistance are the norm. **The administrative and logistical needs must be clearly identified and provided for.** Wherever possible, local administrative infrastructures should be used to implement any response. Some response options require more administration than others; for example, food for work calls for the identification of appropriate projects, selection of people to participate and to supervise the work, and requires considerable logistics capacity to move and distribute food.

The long-term effects of interventions

Most interventions have much wider long-term implications than first realised. There may be some beneficial effects, such as strengthening local infrastructures. However, providing food assistance can have lasting negative effects on food production, market prices of food, leadership and organisation within communities and local government, and longer-term development programmes.

Emergency responses may save lives in the short term but in isolation do little or nothing to make people stronger next time round. **Emergency programmes that are maintained for longer than necessary can undermine attempts to address the underlying causes of food scarcity and famine**.

3.2 Choosing the appropriate response

The choice of response is largely determined by the **severity** and **nature** of food scarcity. In a famine lives are seriously at risk and the immediate objective is therefore to prevent people dying, which may require an emergency intervention.

In contrast, in a situation of food scarcity, the objectives are to protect and support people's livelihoods and thus improve their access to food and prevent the situation worsening. At the same time it may be necessary to take preventive measures to protect health.

The main objectives of responding to a situation of food scarcity or famine are therefore:

- To avoid epidemics and **reduce excess mortality** by taking emergency actions.

- To **support people's livelihoods** by means of income support measures.

- To **protect health and nutrition** by means of public health measures.

To meet these objectives **several combined strategies** are usually needed. The next section links the above objectives with some typical intervention measures. The list is not exhaustive and reflects recent experience in Africa.

Response options

Objective: Avoid epidemics and reduce excess mortality.

Response: Where lives are threatened, speedy actions on several fronts are necessary to avoid further deaths and the spread of infection. In particular, health care measures, such as measles immunisation, vitamin A supplementation, provision of essential drugs and ORS, as well as adequate supplies of clean water, sanitary facilities, shelter and food, may be needed. The order of priority of these needs depends on the situation and the immediate threats to health.

Providing food assistance is only part of the overall response and may be ineffective unless people's other basic needs are met. Part Four of this manual describes types of food distribution programmes. For information about other emergency programmes, in particular, shelter, water and sanitation, see the reading list at the end of the manual.

Objective: Protect and support threatened livelihoods.

Response: Threatened livelihoods make it more difficult for people to acquire the food and other essentials they need. Any response should aim at improving people's access to food, for example:

- **Market interventions**: The provision of low cost or subsidised cereal may ease the effect of high market prices or actual food shortages. Price controls or rationing of food in the market place is usually the responsibility of the government.

- **Food or cash for work**: Work programmes have been successfully used in some countries to ensure that people are able to obtain food, or the money to buy food. These programmes are often 'self-selecting', which means only those who really need assistance volunteer themselves. The timing of these programmes is critical, as they should not interfere with people's normal occupations, particularly with periods of intense agricultural activity. They should be designed to fit in with and complement local self-help initiatives. Food or cash for work programmes require careful planning, organisation, and the necessary tools and other materials to do the work. In many parts of Africa these programmes have been of limited success because of inappropriate and inadequate planning.

- **Exchanging livestock or other resources for food or cash**: In Kenya, Oxfam have implemented successful de-stocking programmes. Pastoralists faced with deteriorating terms of trade (increases in prices of cereals with decreasing prices of livestock) were able to exchange some of their livestock for food. At a later date, Oxfam implemented a re-stocking project.

- **Targeted food distribution**: In situations of food scarcity, free food distributions often create more problems than they solve. However, if those most in need are carefully targeted, food assistance may support people during lean periods and so prevent further economic and nutritional decline. For example, limited food assistance to rural farmers during the 'hungry' season just before the harvest, enables them to undertake necessary agricultural work.

Objective: Protect health and nutrition.

Response: Clean water, sanitation and basic health care based on a primary health care approach and health education are pre-requisites for ensuring good health and are the backbone of all public health programmes.

In normal times there may be various constraints that limit the provision of primary health care. This means that people are more vulnerable to poor health in times of food scarcity and famine, as they are relatively unprotected. The

49

situation may be exacerbated by conditions found in camps of displaced people, such as overcrowding, poor water and inadequate sanitation, which increase exposure to infection. Because of the permanent nature of public health programmes, it is vital that any temporary measures to improve water, sanitation or basic health care, fit in and strengthen any existing public health programme.

When to distribute food assistance

The appropriate response to a situation of food scarcity is not necessarily to distribute food. There are **two main purposes** of food distribution: to support nutrition or give economic support. Where people have very little or no access to food it is essential to provide food rations that cover their total nutritional requirements. For example, where people have recently become refugees, or are destitute and living in makeshift camps.

Food can also be distributed to people so that they can conserve their resources in order to plant for the next harvest or maintain their herds of livestock. This is a way of supporting livelihoods. This may be appropriate where people are selling off vital assets in order to obtain food for their families. By supporting people at this stage, they are able to stay in their own homes, thereby avoiding the greater health risks found in relief camps.

In times of food scarcity, if people are able to obtain some food for themselves, a food distribution may provide both nutritional and economic support. Nutritional support may be necessary for infants and young children and pregnant and lactating mothers, who need more protein and energy rich foods than other groups in the community. If the nutritional quality and quantity of their diet deteriorates they are liable to become malnourished and their health may suffer.

However, where people are not totally dependent on food aid, it is more difficult to decide whether or not to give food. This is because any assessment of the shortfall in people's food requirements will inevitably be a crude estimate, yet errors in this estimate may have serious negative consequences. Too little food could contribute to malnutrition, while too much food is also harmful, for a variety of reasons. The harmful consequences of food distribution may include:

- Drawing people away from their usual pattern of life and creating unrealistic expectations.

- Changing attitudes and hindering grassroots development.

- Depressing prices for food in local markets and affecting local livelihoods.

- Producing conflicts in the wider community between those who receive and those who do not.

- Producing conflict and resentment between the development agency and local people, by putting the agency in an authoritarian role.

- Food distribution being used for political purposes.

3.3 Targeting

Targeting restricts the coverage of an intervention to those who are perceived to be most in need. Thus, targeting directs interventions at **specific areas** (regions, towns, villages, or camps) or to **groups of people** who are worst affected by food scarcity and famine.

As well as making sure the interventions reach the right people, targeting also ensures that those who do not need assistance are excluded from the programme. This reduces the financial costs of the intervention – as long as the costs of targeting are less than the costs of including everybody in the intervention.

Targeting may also limit the known harmful affects associated with external emergency relief, such as undermining development programmes or traditional community support structures. However, in many situations, targeting may be politically too sensitive, or even totally unacceptable.

When resources are scarce, targeting is clearly a **political issue**, as targeting decisions may be made in order to secure political support rather than to assist the poor, who rarely have any means of exerting political pressure. Efforts to target only the poor with valuable resources frequently encounter enormous opposition. For example, drought and subsequent food scarcity will have some effect on most social and occupational groups, even though the effects will vary and only some groups will be in danger of losing their livelihoods or suffering undernutrition. All groups affected will feel entitled to some of the scarce resources and so there may be pressure from the politically stronger groups to obtain a share. This reinforces the need for and importance of a good assessment in demonstrating where the actual needs are, and also in finding solutions to targeting problems, such as other means of supporting vulnerable groups which involve self-selection. Remember, a poorly targeted programme could result in the better-off growing fatter at the expense of the poor.

Identifying the specific areas which have the highest priority for intervention is known as **geographical targeting.** Within these areas, the entire population may be targeted for interventions – **general or universal targeting** – or only selected individuals, households or groups – **selective targeting**.

Geographical targeting

Agencies usually decide where they wish to work. This is often the result of requests for assistance or advice from government, followed by the agency's own assessments.

Experience has shown that relief interventions are not always concentrated in the areas of greatest need, but are implemented where access is easiest and also where people have more political power and are able to express their needs for assistance most strongly.

Geographical targeting of food aid should depend on where the need is perceived to be greatest, according to the results of assessments and other sources of information. These decisions are judgments based on all available information about food scarcity and its impact. The use of single indicators, such as nutritional status, to prioritise geographical areas is inappropriate. Comparisons between figures for rates of malnutrition in different areas give a false sense of precision and other relevant information about needs may be ignored. Also, the work required to collect accurate estimates of the rate of malnutrition in all areas of interest is likely to be impractical in terms of time and resources. Remember, too, when comparing rates of malnutrition from sample surveys, the methods used must be comparable and proper statistical tests should be applied (see Appendix 4).

Nutrition data may be useful in confirming other findings, and in this way can contribute to making more informed decisions about targeting. But nutrition data alone should not be used as the criterion for deciding which areas are most in need of food.

General targeting

General or universal targeting includes everybody in the intervention. A good example is the emergency distribution of food rations to people in a relief camp. For ease of distribution, everybody receives the same food ration despite their varying nutritional needs, and the ration is based on the average nutritional requirements of the entire population.

In some situations of food scarcity, entire communities may have been affected and thus everyone feels entitled to their share of the externally provided resources, in which case selective targeting may be controversial. However, general targeting will reduce the share that is allocated to the most vulnerable groups.

General targeting of food is appropriate where everybody appears to be **equally affected**, such as a group of refugees recently arrived in a camp. It may also be necessary where the administrative infrastructure to implement selective targeting is extremely weak or non-existent, because general targeting is far easier to administer.

Selective targeting

There are a number of ways in which individuals or households may be selected for inclusion in a particular intervention. Selective targeting involves

establishing criteria to identify those individuals or households who qualify; **screening** the entire population to find and register all those eligible; and **establishing systems** for reaching those selected. The system must allow others who qualify to be admitted to the programme once it is set up, and people whose circumstances change for the better to be discharged.

Criteria for selection

The criteria used to select people should be **associated with the objectives of the intervention**. For example, if the objective is to prevent death from measles, the target group will be those age groups who are particularly vulnerable, such as the under-fives.

The criteria for selection should also be **easily measured or assessed**, otherwise errors will result in many vulnerable people being missed out while others who are less in need are included. A good example is the use of anthropometry to identify severely malnourished children for admission to a therapeutic feeding programme. Nutritional status is used as the admission criteria to supplementary and therapeutic feeding programmes in famine and refugee camps. Children are discharged from these programmes once they regain weight and their nutritional status improves (see Sections 4.3 and 4.4 Supplementary and Therapeutic Feeding Programmes). Nutritional interventions are often targeted at those who are less able to meet their relatively greater nutritional needs, such as malnourished children, pregnant and lactating women, the sick and the elderly.

Socio-economic characteristics, such as income or wealth, are more difficult to apply as criteria for targeting. Vulnerable or poorer households cannot be identified by assessing a single criterion, because a multitude of factors influence how poor they are. For example, a man with regular paid work may appear to have adequate resources, but he may be responsible for many dependents, in which case his income may be insufficient for their needs.

Where several factors are used to identify people in need, the targeting system becomes complicated and difficult to administer. Also, its implementation and effectiveness can cause controversy.

In general, **selective targeting is to be avoided**, because the institutional and logistical capacity needed are beyond the resources of most agencies, particularly in times of food scarcity and famine. Also, it is potentially damaging to relations between the community and the agency when the agency becomes involved in identifying beneficiaries.

Selection by community representatives

In times of food scarcity, when people are still living at home, it is difficult for agency staff to make an accurate assessment of the varying needs within a

53

community for the purposes of targeting. The government may have estimated the total food shortfall for a region, but needs within the region, and even within villages, are likely to vary considerably.

If households are to be selected within a community the decision as to which households should receive food is best taken by local representatives, providing community leadership is intact, as they have a far better knowledge of individual circumstances than have agency staff.

The operating agency should, however, **carefully monitor the targeted distribution** to check who is getting food, why they have been targeted and what they are getting. The main reason for this is to ensure that all marginalised groups have been included, and also that the targeting is not so broad that the amounts of food received per family are very small. It is particularly important to make sure that women are not being unfairly treated; if possible, women should be involved in the distribution of food.

Targeting of limited resources

The priority in any famine situation is to provide an adequate food ration for **everybody** in need. However, in extreme famine situations, where the relief system has failed to provide an adequate ration, agencies have used nutritional status to direct what little food they had available to families whose children were malnourished.

Giving food on this basis is far from satisfactory and is unfair to other families whose children are just above the anthropometric cut-off point or more than five years old, or to people who have no children. It can cause enormous resentment, and in extremely bad situations may even force families to starve their children in order to ensure the whole family qualifies for food aid.

In this dire situation, every effort must be made to try and remedy the underlying failure of the relief system, to prevent more children becoming severely malnourished and at greater risk of dying. The decisions in such a situation are extremely difficult to make, and there must be full consultation with community representatives, local government, agency head offices and any other relevant parties.

Self-selection

It is possible for people to decide for themselves whether or not to be included in an intervention, depending on whether they want assistance and what they must do in order to get it. For example, food or cash for work may only be attractive to those able and willing to work for the wages or food offered. A further example is the provision of subsidised food which may be nutritionally adequate but is thought a poor substitute for the preferred staple food, such as red sorghum in place of white sorghum.

The role of the agency

Your **agency's role** in any response will depend on several factors, including the response of government and other agencies, the resources available and the logistical and administrative constraints of becoming operational. Oxfam traditionally channels support through local institutions but, in the absence of local agencies, has also at times become operational.

Apart from becoming involved in actual interventions, the findings from your assessment may play a key role in terms of **advocacy**; alerting the wider community to the situation in order to secure the necessary resources and response.

PART FOUR:

FOOD DISTRIBUTION

If, as a result of your assessment of the situation, you have decided that it is necessary to distribute food, there are still more decisions to be made. In this part of the book, in Section 4.1, we first of all look at some of the problems that can occur in the course of a food distribution, and the different ways food might be distributed. We then look in detail at three types of food distribution: 4.2 deals with general food rations, 4.3 with supplementary feeding programmes and 4.4 with therapeutic feeding programmes.

4.1 Some problems that might occur

Food distribution needs a high degree of organisation and management. Experience shows that giving food on a regular basis to a home-based population is fraught with logistical and other managerial problems. Long delays in planned food distribution schedules are common and the rations eventually given rarely match the rations that were previously planned. Be aware of the difficulties of the task ahead.

You could face problems at any one of the various stages of food distribution:

- Assessing the food requirements and planning an appropriate ration.

- Procuring suitable food, possibly from different sources.

- Arranging appropriate transport for the existing road conditions.

- Arranging adequate storage where required.

- Deciding how the food should be targeted.

- Setting up an appropriate system of distribution and possibly registering the population.

- Monitoring the food distribution system and the effect of distribution on the nutritional status of those receiving food.

- Stopping the distribution.

- Minimising the harmful consequences of giving food aid.

This manual does not cover many of the logistical issues raised in this list. Before you begin a food distribution ask yourself two questions:

- **Why do these people need food now?** and

- **What else could we be doing to support them?**

The decision whether or not to distribute food is closely linked to deciding **who should receive food**; see p.50 for the purposes of food distribution, and Section 3.3 for a discussion of targeting.

Types of food distribution

There are four main types of food distribution:

- **General food rations** are given to **everybody** in the population. In any situation the provision of food for all those affected must be the priority.

  Where refugees and the internally displaced have no other source of food, the general ration must cover their **total nutritional requirements**. A simple ration would include a staple food such as sorghum, wheat or rice, plus oil and beans or lentils.

  In times of food scarcity, if people still have access to some food, the ration they receive may consist of a staple food only. In this situation total nutritional support is not essential. When the ration consists of a staple food only it is sometimes called a **basic ration.**

- **Complementary rations** are foods that **complement the nutritional quality** of the diet or basic ration, for example, beans, lentils, oil and specially processed foods (fortified cereals and porridge mixes). These foods contribute to a more nutritionally balanced diet and make it more palatable. Complementary rations are often included as part of the general ration where people have no other source of food.

- **Supplementary feeding programmes** are intended to supplement the diets of **nutritionally vulnerable groups**, such as infants, young children, pregnant and lactating mothers.

- **Therapeutic feeding programmes** are intended to rehabilitate the most **seriously malnourished children** through intensive feeding and health care.

Supplementary and therapeutic feeding programmes are sometimes called **selective feeding programmes.** Selective feeding is a low priority and should only be undertaken in a life-threatening emergency once the following have been established:

- Access to an adequate diet or general ration.

- Access to clean water.

- Immunisation against measles.

- Vitamin A supplementation of all children under five where the population is in danger of developing vitamin A deficiency.

These actions will ultimately save more lives than selective feeding. (However, see also page 54 for a discussion of targeting of limited resources.)

4.2 General food rations

The main aim of a general food ration is to provide people with a source of nutritious food, to prevent undernutrition. Provision of free food also acts as a form of economic support to people whose livelihoods are weakened by food scarcity. But remember that free food distributions can have negative consequences (see page 50).

There are four main groups of people to whom general rations may appropriately be distributed: refugees, internally displaced, home-based communities, and transhumant pastoralists and nomads. Refugees and the internally displaced may have gathered in camps, and may be totally dependent on food aid as their sole source of food. Home-based and nomadic people may only need support for a limited period – maybe until the next harvest.

Estimating population size

Estimates of the number of people who need food are essential in order to calculate requirements, but are notoriously difficult to obtain. In a refugee camp, a rough estimate may be made by mapping the area and counting houses. Where a population is home-based, start with census data. If it is out-of-date, check it with additional data, such as community registration lists for tax purposes, community services, subsidised food distributions, and veterinary or other services.

During visits to villages, ask village leaders to list all the families in their tribe or village. Make a rough house count to check numbers and draw a rough sketch map of the area.

When calculating population size, remember to consider new arrivals or out-migration, and regularly review your initial population estimates.

Foods for a general ration

The general ration should include:

- A staple food, such as wheat, maize, sorghum or rice, to provide the bulk of protein and energy.

- Vegetable or butter oil, to provide a concentrated source of energy and make the ration more palatable.

- Beans or lentils to increase the amount of protein in the ration. Processed foods, such as fortified blends of cereals and beans (corn soya milk or soya fortified sorghum grits) may be used as an alternative to beans and lentils in an emergency (Appendix 8).

The cereal, dried peas or beans should be of a type that people are accustomed to eating. Where people are totally dependent on food aid, other foods should be given to make the diet more palatable, such as, salt, spices, tea or coffee, and sugar. Vitamin and mineral deficiencies have been found among refugee populations in Africa who have been dependent on food rations for long periods. These deficiencies have serious consequences for health and can even cause death. See Appendix 7 for more information on vitamin and mineral deficiencies.

Milling

Whole grain cereals have better keeping qualities than milled flours and therefore cereals are usually provided as whole grain, which must be milled either before distribution or by the people who receive it.

Milling may cause a loss of up to ten per cent of the original total weight, depending on the 'extraction' rate. The extraction rate is lower if the grain is milled by hand or at a local mill. Another consideration is whether people can afford the additional cost of milling at the local mill.

The extra cost of milling and the losses incurred should be allowed for when calculating budgets and ration sizes. Increases in ration size of between five and ten per cent may be needed.

Source of food

Food for general rations are usually provided by the government, bi-lateral donors, the EEC, or the United Nations via the World Food Programme or the UN High Commissioner for Refugees.

Whenever possible, supplies of food should be bought in the country itself, or in neighbouring countries, from areas where there are surpluses. This clearly has the effect of stimulating local economies, and is preferable to importing the grain surpluses of rich countries.

The amount and type of food in a general ration

It is impractical to assess the precise nutritional needs of individuals and to provide different rations according to those needs. It is also difficult to define average energy requirements, as they vary according to body size and growth, health status and physical activity.

The United Nations World Food Programme and High Commissioner for

Refugees recommend a minimum of **1900Kcal** per person per day (PPPD). This should be increased if:

- A high proportion of children are malnourished, and adults also appear to be in a poor state of health and nutrition.

- People are doing manual work or other physical exercise.

- People are exposed to the cold (increase the ration by five per cent for every 5°C decrease in temperature below 20°C).

- There is a high proportion of people who have relatively greater nutritional requirements e.g. adult males doing physically demanding work, pregnant and lactating mothers, children and adolescents.

Food rations should be nutritionally well balanced, especially if they are the only source of food available. **In a balanced ration, protein should provide 12.5 per cent of total energy and fat should provide at least 10.0 per cent of total energy.**

To calculate the amount of protein needed to provide 12.5 per cent of total energy (1900Kcal):

12.5% of total energy =
    (1900/100) x 12.5 = 237.5Kcal

So protein should provide about 240Kcal of a 1900Kcal ration.
1g protein gives 4Kcal, so, 240Kcal is equal to:
    240/4 = 60g protein

A ration of 1900Kcal should therefore contain 60g protein, to provide 12.5 per cent of total energy. Both the cereal and the beans contain protein, so 60g protein could be provided by 400g cereals and 50g beans (see Table 4).

The fat content of the ration may be calculated in a similar way (1g fat gives 9Kcal). **A ration of 1900Kcal should contain 22g fat**, which provides 10.4 per cent of total energy.

Weight g	Food	Energy Kcal	Protein g	Fat
350–500	**CEREAL**	1155–1650	35–55	7–8
20–40	**OIL**	180–360	0	178–356
50–100	**BEANS**	175–350	10–20	1–2

Table 4: Range of food quantities for a general ration (per person per day)

By varying combinations of these foods, rations with different energy and nutrient contents can be calculated. If the energy content of the ration is increased, the amount of protein and fat should be increased proportionately. The energy and nutrient content of common foods are shown in Appendix 8.

You may not have all the recommended food to hand. Where individual items in the ration basket are missing they should be substituted for by increasing the amounts of other foods. If no oil is available, substitute twice the amount of beans or sugar, e.g. 50g oil could be substituted with 100g sugar. If there are no beans or lentils in the ration, substitute with the same quantity of fortified blends of cereals and beans (CSM, ICSM).

The size of the ration can be reduced if people are able to obtain food from other sources. In situations of limited food availability, the ration should be based on the estimated total food deficit in the community for a given period of time. This estimate is likely to be extremely crude and based on factors such as harvest shortfall or predicted availability of food in the market. It is vital that other sources of food and coping strategies are also taken into account (see Sections 2.1.2 and 2.1.3).

Where the food scarcity problem is one of limited access on the part of certain groups to the available food, it is unrealistic to make quantitative estimates of loss in entitlements. However, a detailed description of how different groups are affected will help in deciding the composition of the ration and factors such as frequency and duration of distribution.

In a situation of loss of entitlements, a single commodity ration consisting of cereals may be more appropriate than a mixed food basket, unless there are serious nutritional problems in the community. In fact, most situations of food scarcity are caused by a combination of limited food availability and loss of entitlements.

Monthly food requirement

As a rough guide, the monthly requirement of food for 1,000 people is 15 metric tonnes (500g PPPD). Losses of food during transport, storage and distribution are inevitable. An additional five per cent should be added the ration to allow for this (15.75MT per month for 1,000 people).

Frequency of distribution

This partly depends on logistical constraints but also on what is most suitable from the point of view of the people receiving the food. Longer intervals between distributions frequently lead to greater delays, as more food must be pre-positioned prior to the distribution. However, longer intervals may suit people better if they are home-based, as they have to travel less in order to collect their rations.

Weight is also a factor to consider; two adults may be able to carry one month's ration for a family of five (60kg). People may own donkeys they can use for transport.

It is important to maintain regularity. If the distribution schedule is not adhered to, the nutritional objectives of providing the food will not be met, irrespective of whether there is a further decline in nutritional status or not. People quickly lose confidence in irregular distributions and may settle near the distribution site to ensure they are present when food is given out, which could have severe consequences on health (see page 13).

In situations of food scarcity, consider the timing of food distribution in relation to the local agricultural season. It may be appropriate to organise a 'one-off' distribution, equivalent to full rations for one or two months, that will support people before the harvest. People are then able to pursue their normal agricultural work, confident they have food to last until the harvest is in.

Organisation

Usually the general ration distribution is coordinated by government administration or international agencies. Non-governmental agencies are involved when there is an obvious need for them to 'fill gaps' caused by failures in the relief system. Or they may become involved during times of political instability when donors prefer to channel their food through an agency that has experience of working in a particular area or with a particular group of people.

Most home-based communities or groups of transhumant pastoralists have well-developed systems of organisation and leadership. Wherever possible, these existing systems should be used to organise and implement the food distribution. This may be especially appropriate in times of food scarcity if food has to be carefully directed to those in greatest need. It is important to ensure women are consulted and if possible involved in food distribution. (*Practical Guide to Registration* (see Further Reading) gives information about community-managed distribution of relief supplies.)

Ending a distribution

Do not start an 'open-ended' food distribution programme. Before a programme is started either:

● Decide how long the programme is to last, and agree on criteria for keeping it open should the need arise; or

● Decide on criteria for closure which will be reviewed at a certain date.

The first option is preferable as it emphasises that the programme is of limited duration.

Monitoring

When beginning a food distribution programme, it is important to set up monitoring systems. Monitoring of the food distribution should include:

- Assessing the **immediate impact on nutrition and health** (rates of malnutrition, mortality rates) and factors affecting this.

- Monitoring the **general situation** (people's access to food, market conditions, harvest prospects).

- Monitoring the **efficiency** of the programme (coverage, attendance, problems).

This information should be used for programme management – making decisions about targeting, screening and closure. (See Section 2.2 for assessment methods.)

4.3 Supplementary feeding programmes

Supplementary feeding is common throughout the developing world, although studies have repeatedly shown the limited impact of supplementary feeding programmes on growth (stature). This is partly because supplementary feeding is a direct nutrition intervention responding to the immediate problem of food availability, but does nothing to address the underlying causes of malnutrition linked with low entitlements and poverty. The effectiveness of supplementary feeding is now controversial, to say the least. The role of supplementary feeding in emergencies has been criticised for various reasons:

- In emergencies, supplementary feeding may be appealing to operational agencies because it appears to be a very obvious and practical response to the needs of the most vulnerable in the community – malnourished children. This may divert attention and resources away from the more pressing priorities which indirectly may have greater impact on health and nutrition, such as establishing a clean water supply or an adequate general ration.

- Supplementary feeding in emergencies is often organised in a way that suggests programme staff 'know best'; which takes responsibility for child health away from mothers and leaves little room for community participation in dealing with nutritional problems.

- Even in relief camps, where feeding centres are close to where people are living, programme coverage tends to be low and attendance by those registered in the programme is often poor.

You need to consider all these factors carefully, before deciding to implement a supplementary feeding programme. It might be preferable to include extra dry rations suitable for weaning of infants and young children as part of the general ration. This would eliminate the need for a separate supplementary feeding programme.

However, there is an important difference between supplementary feeding in emergencies and non-emergency situations. In emergencies, the aim of supplementary feeding is principally to promote weight gain among already malnourished children, which may be achieved within a relatively short period of time (2 to 3 months). In non-emergencies, the focus has been on promoting growth of all children, not only the malnourished, which takes years rather than months to achieve. Also, beyond the first two or three years of life, growth failure (shortness) may be irreversible.

Supplementary and therapeutic feeding are described in detail in *Selective Feeding Programmes: Oxfam Practical Health Guide 1* (see Further Reading).

The aims of supplementary feeding

In emergencies such as famine or refugee situations, the aim of supplementary feeding is to treat children who are already malnourished rather than to prevent malnutrition. This is achieved by providing nourishing food in addition to the normal diet. **To be effective the extra rations must be additional to, and not a substitute for, the normal diet.**

Supplementary feeding should be part of a larger health care programme, including immunisation, vitamin A supplementation and treatment of diarrhoea and other infections.

Organisation of supplementary feeding programmes

Supplementary food may be provided as uncooked food rations given to the mother to prepare for the child at home (**dry rations**), or as cooked food, which is eaten by the child under supervision in a feeding centre (**wet rations**).

Unless children are severely malnourished, it is always preferable to provide dry rations for mothers to prepare at home because daily visits to feeding centres are very disruptive to people's lives, which often results in poor attendance and failure of the children to gain weight. Daily gatherings of children in feeding shelters increase the risk of the transmission of infection. Moderate malnutrition is not life-threatening and daily supervision of child feeding should not be necessary.

Where people are home-based, it may be logistically difficult to provide sufficient numbers of centres and inevitably access to shelter will be limited to those living close by.

Also, wet feeding requires greater resources than dry feeding; more equipment, better facilities, a regular supply of fuel and water, and staff to manage and supervise the programme.

As far as possible, the programme should be organised and supervised by people from the community or camp. This is good for morale, particularly as the improvement in the health of children may be the first obvious sign of recovery in the community.

Admission criteria

People who would qualify for admission to supplementary feeding programmes include:

- Moderately malnourished children (70 per cent to below 80 per cent of the reference median weight for height).

- Severely malnourished children (less than 70 per cent weight for height), where there are no facilities for therapeutic feeding.

- Children who are around 80 per cent WFH, who have other health problems.

- Children discharged from therapeutic feeding programmes.

- Orphans and unaccompanied children.

- Pregnant and lactating women.

- Undernourished adults with serious illness such as TB.

- The elderly.

It may be appropriate to provide supplementary feeding for all infants and children aged five and under, where there are additional nutritional risks, such as a recent measles epidemic, a high rate of acute malnutrition, or a general ration or diet which is of low nutritional value. In the past, selective feeding programmes have usually been set up for children of five and under (less than 110cm), although surveys show that children aged three years and below suffer higher rates of acute malnutrition. The choice of admission criteria and age cut-off points depends partly on the available resources. If resources allow, all children under three years of age should be admitted, plus any child, regardless of age, less that 80 per cent weight for height. If resources are limited, then numbers must be reduced, for example, by admitting only those children under five years of age who are less than 75 per cent weight for height. The admission criteria may be altered as the situation changes.

Children should be discharged from supplementary feeding programmes when they are healthy, active, have a good appetite and their nutritional status is above 85 per cent weight for height.

Screening

In order to identify those who are eligible for admission, everybody in the population should be screened. This may involve visiting every house or tent.

To find children less than five years old, children should be measured, using a measuring stick or simple height arch for children to walk under (115cm high). The average height of normal five-year-olds is 110cm; for screening purposes, identify all those less than 115cm tall, which allows a safety margin. Malnourished children can be identified by measuring the nutritional status of those children less than 115cm. To speed this process up, divide it into two stages; first, measure the arm circumference (MUAC) of every child and only refer those with a MUAC less than 14cm to the second stage, which is actual weighing and height measurement. This reduces the numbers of children to be weighed and measured, which is a considerably slower and more cumbersome process (see Section 2.2.3).

Food for supplementary feeding

Food given in supplementary feeding programmes should be nutritionally adequate for weaning infants and for children under five years old, and should also be palatable. It should be **energy dense** (see below), **high in protein** (at least 12 per cent of the total energy should be protein), and should be a good source of **essential vitamins** and **minerals**.

Children who are malnourished need additional food of high nutritional value for 'catch-up' growth and weight gain. Food that is nutritionally adequate for adults is often inadequate for malnourished children, who, for example, need an increased ratio of protein to energy in their diet.

Acceptability is very important; the food should be tasty but not too spicy nor too sweet, and suitable for young children – a semi-liquid porridge. It should be quick and simple to prepare, if given for home consumption, and based on local foods where possible. It should have no associated health risks (see page 67 for the serious health risks of dried skimmed milk powder).

The importance of energy dense foods

It is important that the food given is **'energy dense'** and contains adequate amounts of protein. Young children have small appetites. If food is bulky but contains few nutrients the child will lose its appetite and become full before it has eaten enough to satisfy its nutritional needs.

A food is said to be energy dense if more than 20 per cent of total energy is from fat. This means that dry foods such as porridge mix or biscuits should contain at least 10g of fat per 100g.

Dry weight per 100g	Energy Kcal	Per cent of total energy
10g fat	90	21
13g protein	52	12
78g carbohydrate	293	67
Total energy	435	100

Table 5: Typical composition of high energy/high protein biscuits

Appropriate high energy drinks (high energy milk) and porridges may be made from specially processed or blended foods (porridge mixes such as Corn Soya Milk (CSM), *faffa*), dried milk powder, flour and oil. Sugar is added to improve taste and increase energy. **High energy drinks must contain 1Kcal per ml (100Kcal per 100mls).**

Foods given to mothers to take away and prepare at home should also be energy dense. This is achieved by preparing a 'pre-mix' of dry ingredients (cereal flour, bean flour, milk powder, CSM, or sugar) to which oil is added. Commercially processed porridge mixes or blended foods are produced by combining cereal flour, ground peas or beans and milk powder. They are usually fortified with vitamins and minerals. Instant porridge mixes, such as Instant Corn Soya Milk (ICSM), are precooked during processing and therefore do not need long cooking, thus conserving fuel.

The nutritional composition of blended foods makes them suitable for use as a weaning food. However, **oil must be added** to increase the energy density. Blended foods are produced in some developing countries and may be useful for supplementary feeding in emergencies. In Ethiopia, production of the local weaning food, *faffa*, was expanded to cope with demands during the 1984/1985 famine. (Recipes for drinks, porridges and pre-mixes are given in Appendix 11.)

The dangers of dried skimmed milk powder

Dried skimmed milk (DSM) or dried whole milk (DWM) have been common in selective feeding programmes in the past, because dried milk is often the only high protein food freely available to operational agencies.

However, **the distribution of dried milk powder is potentially dangerous to health and nutrition** because, once reconstituted with water, DSM is an excellent environment for the growth of food-poisoning bacteria. Bacteria present on hands, in water and on kitchen tools are able to multiply quickly in prepared DSM to dangerously high levels, particularly if the water is not boiled beforehand or if the reconstituted milk is kept for several hours unrefrigerated.

Milk contaminated with bacteria may cause sickness and diarrhoea among infants and young children, which trigger malnutrition or make it worse. Also, dried milk powder may be used by mothers as a substitute for breast milk. This can have lethal consequences for babies, because of the problems associated with poor food hygiene discussed above, and also because the milk may not be prepared in the correct concentration, leading either to undernutrition or problems of digesting highly concentrated milk.

DSM contains none of the fat of whole milk and is therefore lower in energy, and also contains none of the fat soluble vitamins found in whole milk (vitamins A and D). DSM may be fortified with these vitamins during processing, but this is not always the case. DSM is not an energy dense food and therefore is inappropriate for supplementary feeding, unless extra oil is mixed with it.

Because of the dangers of using DSM incorrectly it is very important to follow certain policy guidelines regarding its use:

- DSM that is not fortified with vitamin A should not be used. If no information about fortification is available assume that it is not fortified.

- DSM should not be distributed on its own as a dry powder in any type of food distribution.

- A pre-mix of DSM, plus oil, cereal flour and other ingredients may be used in the following situations:

    Selective feeding of infants and young children (wet and dry).

    Complementary rations where there are no peas, beans or lentils available and milk is traditionally a very common item in the diet (consumed daily).

- Preparation of pre-mix must be as hygienic as possible; hands, equipment and utensils must be clean.

- The water must be from a safe source or treated and only 'safe' water must be used.

You may be under pressure to distribute DSM because it is often readily available, and is a good source of protein, which may be lacking in the general diet or ration. People who often drink milk ask for milk powder as they can substitute it for fresh milk. People may also want it because it is a 'high status' food – something only rich people can afford. However, **none of these reasons justify the distribution of DSM.**

The importance of breast feeding

Breast feeding should continue for as long as possible and at least until the second year of life. Breast milk is the most nourishing and clean food for infants and gives them protection against many infectious diseases. Breast milk is sufficient on its own to nourish a baby until the age of six months, when other foods should be introduced.

Where mothers are having difficulty breast feeding, they must be helped and supported by giving them extra food and spending time patiently encouraging them and trying to find out the cause of the problem.

Where breast feeding is not possible for the mother, or if the infant is unaccompanied, the best solution is to find other women who are prepared to breast feed children other than their own. Some compensation should be considered for their time and help.

As a last resort use a spoon and cup for feeding, but **NEVER** use an infant feeding bottle. **BOTTLE FEEDING IS DANGEROUS** – bacteria grow and multiply in the conditions found in feeding bottles and may cause diarrhoea. Feeding bottles are much harder to keep clean than a cup and spoon.

The amount of food to give

A supplementary ration usually aims to provide an extra **500 to 800Kcal per person per day (PPPD)**. In a wet feeding centre, extra food should be provided for the mother or other attendant.

A take-home ration should be at least doubled to allow for sharing with others in the family – **1000 to 1600Kcal PPPD**. In situations where the general ration is irregular or otherwise inadequate these amounts should be increased.

As the supplementary ration is extra to the normal diet, it is best eaten as two or three small extra meals 'in-between' other regular meals. An infant is unable to eat much more than 300 to 400Kcal without becoming full and so would have to stay in the wet feeding centre for a few hours in order to eat the ration. An alternative is for the children to attend the centre twice each day.

Where the food is taken home, the child's feeding times are the responsibility of the mother. Explain clearly that the food supplement is inadequate on its own and must be **additional** to the normal diet.

Monitoring the programme

A simple system for monitoring the programme is necessary. Keep a **register** recording basic information for each person admitted to the programme, including registration number, name, age, sex, weight, height, arm circumference, and date of admission. All admissions, transfers, discharges and deaths, with their respective dates, must be recorded in the register.

Individual **record cards** should show the same basic information as found in the register. They should be used to record continuous information about the child, including weight, rations received by the child, and any other medical treatment.

If the family already has a general ration card, this could be used to record the receipt of dry supplementary rations. Alternatively, each child should have an **identity bracelet** with a registration number that corresponds with the number in the register or on their card.

Checking individual attendance on a daily basis is time consuming. A more efficient way of recording attendance rates is a simple head count at the end of each session. Individuals who are failing to attend are identified on fortnightly weighing days and followed up.

Children should be weighed about every two weeks to monitor their weight gain.

Positive weight gain = 8g to 10g per kg body weight per day.

Therefore a child weighing 7.5kg should gain at least 60 to 70g per day or 420 to 490g per week. If a child is not gaining weight satisfactorily, it is important to find out the reasons for this (see page 72).

Monthly summary records

It is an aid to effective monitoring to prepare summary records giving the figures for the following:

Total number registered: Children 0-5 years, male and female
Children over 5 years
Pregnant and lactating women
Other adults.

Weight gain: Number and proportion of children (by sex):
– gaining weight
– showing no weight change
– losing weight.

Mortality: Number dying and cause of death.

Admissions/Discharges: Number of new admissions
Number of re-admissions
Number discharged
Number lost to follow-up
Average length of stay of those discharged.

Attendance: Average monthly attendance.

Make comments about the summary statistics and describe important events or interventions that have occurred, such as vitamin A supplementation or sudden departure of large numbers of people. Pay attention to differences by gender.

Closure of the programme

Emergency supplementary feeding is generally no longer appropriate if the level of acute malnutrition has dropped below ten per cent of the reference median weight for height. However, other factors should also be considered, such as the size, quality and regularity of the general ration or diet and the possible seasonal fluctuations in nutritional status, also the prevalence of communicable diseases such as measles or diarrhoea.

Follow-up surveys

Nutrition surveys should be undertaken regularly to monitor levels of malnutrition. This is especially important if the overall situation is unstable and conditions are liable to deteriorate. Additional information should be collected in order to understand the cause of any changes in the rate of malnutrition (see Part Two: Assessments and Surveys).

Surveys should also assess programme coverage: the proportion of malnourished children found in the survey who are registered for supplementary feeding.

Wider aspects of the programme

The supplementary feeding programme should be closely linked to other health measures, including measles immunisation, vitamin A supplementation and screening for other health problems, such as diarrhoea and acute respiratory infections. An effective referral system between the different services should be in operation.

Feeding centres may act as a focal point for other activities, particularly those that involve women, such as community kitchens, income generation activities (handcrafts, pottery, poultry rearing, firewood collecting), vegetable growing, literacy and other educational classes.

Problems of supplementary feeding programmes

Supplementary feeding programmes take up considerable time and resources that may be better spent on other programmes (water, sanitation, shelter, blankets or clothing, immunisation).

Nutrition surveys may indicate that coverage is poor, and only a small proportion of malnourished children are included in the SFP. You should consider whether it might be more appropriate to widen the admission criteria to include all children under three or five years. This requires more food but is easier to administer and organise.

If the attendance at wet feeding programmes is poor, home visits should be made to follow up those children failing to attend regularly. You should consider switching to dry take-home rations instead, if the problem continues.

Children who fail to gain weight should be investigated. Failure to gain weight can be due to a variety of factors, including:

- Poor attendance because of distance from centre, mother at work, inconvenient hours, stigma associated with going to centre, no follow-up of ' defaulters.

- Food unpalatable.

- Inadequate general ration or diet.

- Illness.

- Loss of appetite.

- Supplementary ration eaten (or sold) by family.

Insufficient fuel is a major problem where large numbers of people have settled. The surrounding area will soon become stripped of available wood. One family cooking on a simple wood stove need 5kg wood per day. Wet feeding programmes should use fuel-efficient stoves to prevent wastage. Distribution of fuel or the introduction of fuel efficient stoves should be considered, but may be difficult to implement.

4.4 Therapeutic feeding

The aim of therapeutic feeding is to rehabilitate the most seriously malnourished children. As well as being malnourished these children are often ill and so need appropriate medical care. A therapeutic feeding programme provides both intensive feeding of special foods, and health care.

This section gives only a brief overview of therapeutic feeding, as it is described in detail in *Selective Feeding: Oxfam Practical Health Guide 1* (see Further Reading).

The admission criteria used in therapeutic feeding programmes organised by agencies in relief camps are if a child is below 70 per cent weight for height, or shows signs of kwashiorkor or oedema.

Children may be discharged when they are healthy, active, have a good appetite, are gaining weight steadily and are at least 80 per cent of the reference median weight for height. Children should be referred to the supplementary feeding programme for continued supervision.

Organisation of therapeutic feeding

Minimum facilities for a therapeutic feeding centre in a warm climate are a compound with some shade and a fenced off kitchen area. In cold conditions, a large empty building is necessary.

The centre should have an adequate water supply and sanitation facilities (latrines), and lockable store cupboards or rooms for storing food and equipment. Oxfam feeding kits contain all the equipment necessary, including all cups, plates and other utensils. **INFANT FEEDING BOTTLES SHOULD NEVER BE USED.**

The number of children in one centre should not be more than 60. Adequate supervision of larger numbers is difficult. Each child and attendant should have a space allotted, and a mat should be provided. Clean drinking water, and water for hand-washing, should be available for general use.

All new admissions should be isolated from the other children for the first few days to prevent the spread of infectious diseases, in particular gastro-enteritis, measles, meningitis and whooping cough.

During these first few days of feeding, children are likely to have diarrhoea or may have had diarrhoea prior to admission. They should be fed on half strength high energy milk for the first 24 to 48 hours and full strength milk should be introduced as soon as possible. It is important to maintain feeding during episodes of diarrhoea. Where diarrhoea has caused dehydration, **REMEMBER, ORAL REHYDRATION CAN BE LIFE-SAVING.** Use either the prepackaged oral rehydration solution (ORS) and make up as recommended on the packet, or prepare home-made ORS with the following proportions:

8 level teaspoons sugar
1 level teaspoon salt
· 1 litre boiled and cooled water.

Food for therapeutic feeding

The food given in therapeutic feeding is similar to that given in supplementary feeding: energy dense, high in protein, and a good source of **essential vitamins** and **minerals**, especially vitamin A. It must be in liquid or semi-liquid (porridge) form, to be suitable for young children. (See page 66 on foods for supplementary feeding.) Local foods should be given to add variety to the monotonous diet of drinks and porridge.

Breast feeding must continue while a child is in a therapeutic feeding programme. Where breast feeding has failed the mother should be helped to start again.

Therapeutic feeding should provide several feeds throughout the day and night, that cover the total nutritional requirements of the child. A malnourished child needs at least 150Kcal and 3 to 4g of protein per kg body weight per day. So, a child who weighs 8kg should eat at least:

8 x 150 = 1200Kcal and 8 x 4 = 32g protein.

This is equivalent to 1200ml high energy milk (1 Kcal per ml) which may be given as six feeds of 200ml. Several small feeds are much better than four or five larger feeds (for example, 6a.m., 9a.m., 12 noon, 3p.m., 6p.m., 9p.m. and 12 midnight). Night feeds are important to prevent the blood sugar level dropping dangerously low. They may be logistically difficult to organise, in which case consider distributing biscuits for the midnight feed.

Malnourished children often suffer from loss of appetite. They may need supervision and persuasion to eat the required amount. If they are able to eat more, they should be allowed to. Spend time with mothers, explaining the importance of constantly encouraging malnourished children to eat even when they are reluctant. Feeding can be a slow, laborious task and much perseverance is needed. Sometimes children are encouraged to start eating again by sucking or nibbling on a high energy biscuit. Once children have begun to eat, they will quickly regain their appetite.

If a child is very sick or totally refusing to take feeds a nasogastric tube may be necessary, but in most cases should not be continued for more than 24 hours.

Monitoring

It is clearly important to monitor a therapeutic feeding programme. (See page 69 for monitoring in Supplementary Feeding Programmes.) Children should be weighed at least twice weekly to monitor their weight gain and the results recorded on individual record cards or in a register.

As children get better, they will become less apathetic and irritable and more physically active. Children with kwashiorkor normally lose weight initially as the oedema reduces, followed by a steady increase in weight similar to that shown in marasmic children.

Wider aspects of the programme

Feeding is only one part of the treatment for severely malnourished children; good **medical care** is essential if they are to recover. In areas where malaria is endemic, there is a danger that when malnourished children are fed, they become ill with malaria, because the malaria parasite becomes more active as the blood haemoglobin recovers. Prompt treatment for malaria should be available and, in known endemic areas, all children should be given malaria treatment prophylactically on admission to the programme.

Therapeutic feeding programmes should be integrated into the local health care system as much as possible. In relief camps, the priority health interventions are measles immunisation; control of diarrhoeal diseases; vitamin A supplementation (see Appendix 7); treatment of acute respiratory infections. For details of health interventions in refugee camps refer to *Refugee Health Care: Oxfam Practical Health Guide 2* (see Further Reading).

CONCLUSION

So what next? The emergency is over – or maybe it never was as bad as was feared. Have things returned to normal? It is unlikely that they have. The immediate and obvious effects of famine and food scarcity may be past; people no longer dying in large numbers, and most of them returned to their homes; fewer children malnourished; and the next harvest may look promising.

But underlying these hopeful signs of recovery is the hidden, long-term damage caused by famine and food insecurity. People's assets will be diminished and some may be destitute, with no means of earning a living. Generally, there may be shortages of essential tools or seeds which are necessary if people are to take up their former occupations. Other problems are also likely: squatter camps that seem in danger of becoming permanent; or hundreds of 'orphans' who have become separated from their families.

Emergency interventions rarely just stop. Instead, they evolve with the changing circumstances, and often progress from disaster relief to emergency preparedness or early-warning programmes, and sometimes into long-term development programmes.

However, relief programmes can only be used as springboards for development if, from the beginining, they directly involved those people they were intended to help. From the planning stage onwards, relief programmes must coincide with what people's priorities really are. Badly-thought-out and top-down relief programmes are very unlikely to evolve into a people-centred approach to development; whereas relief strategies that are based on a dialogue with those affected will naturally and more easily grow into appropriate long-term progammes.

The only lasting solutions to problems of food scarcity are to be found with the people themselves; one of the key messages in this book is: **listen and learn** from what they have to say, bearing in mind vested interests (including your own). Remember that, even within communities, different people will have different perspectives and priorities. Community leaders may not always speak in the interests of the people they claim to represent. Seek out those who are most vulnerable to food scarcity and famine; consider who might be unseen or hidden from view, such as women or ethnic minority groups; try to consult people who are clearly affected, but who may be seldom questioned or listened to.

There are no single right answers to the problems of food insecurity. This manual should be used as a source of information and ideas about nutrition in times of food scarcity and famine, rather than as a conclusive guide as to what should be done. Be flexible, explore all the options, no matter how new or novel, and stick by what you learn from the people affected rather than falling back on solutions that have been tried and tested – and frequently failed.

APPENDIX 1

EARLY WARNING

Early warning systems aim to give prior warning of forthcoming food shortages that may adversely affect people. Information is brought together from a variety of sources and regular updates on the situation are produced. Most sustainable early warning systems are based on existing information networks.

The role of agencies

The regular contact which agencies have with project partners and local communities can serve as a 'grassroots' early warning system. People in rural areas often know in advance if food scarcity is going to be more severe than usual, and close contact with them may confirm the predictions of the institutional early warning system.

The use of nutrition data for early warning

Measures of nutrition status such as 'weight for height' and 'weight for age' have been used as part of early warning systems in Africa.

Interpretation: Interpreting the implication of nutrition figures is not easy. Rates of malnutrition are better understood if compared with previous seasonal patterns in the same area (as long as the same methods were used for collecting data). Other information about the influences on nutrition should be looked at to help explain why the figures have changed or stayed the same (see Section 2.4: Analysing and interpreting your findings).

Prediction: In normal years it may be possible to predict patterns of malnutrition according to the season, for example, malnutrition may increase during the 'hungry season' just before the harvest. Departures from this normal seasonal pattern may be used to confirm the effects of unusual events, such as drought and failed harvest.

Planning: Specific rates of malnutrition should not be used as automatic 'triggers' for relief programmes, such as supplementary feeding programmes. The best use of nutrition data is to confirm other findings. Estimates of malnutrition looked at in isolation from other information may not mean very much.

Cost of collecting data: A nutrition surveillance system based on regular surveys is expensive to set up and maintain. This cost may be reduced by including nutritional surveillance as part of existing programmes e.g. mother and child health care. However, in many Sahelian countries these types of programmes are not well developed or only reach a proportion of the population, and so would tend to bias the results.

Despite these problems, there are positive points about collecting nutritional data. Nutritional status is one of the few indicators of the health and well-being of the community that is relatively easy to measure. Also, the collection of nutrition data brings the survey team into direct contact with local people, sometimes in their own homes. This is a valuable opportunity to gain an understanding of people's perceptions of their situation.

APPENDIX 2

WEALTH RANKING

Wealth ranking is a way of learning about and understanding people's perceptions of the differences in wealth between groups in the community.

There are three stages in wealth ranking:

1. A meeting with local representatives to draw up a list of households.

2. Ranking of households by each of two or three 'key' informants, followed by a discussion about the wealth characteristics of each wealth group.

3. Calculation of the average wealth score for each family and division of households into wealth strata.

Stage 1: Meeting with a group of local representatives

1. Discuss local concepts of wealth and decide on a local word or phrase that reflects this.

2. Discuss what constitutes a single household and make a list of all households in the community. If there are more than 100 households in the community, it will be difficult for the informants to rank them. Therefore, select a smaller sub-sample. For example, the households with malnourished children may be a sub-sample of interest. Write the name of each household on a small card or piece of paper.

3. Choose three or four people from the community to be informants. They should know the community well and be from various social groupings, for example, a farmer, someone with paid work, a merchant. Ideally, two of the four should be women. Leaders and officials should be avoided.

Stage 2: Discussion with each of the informants

4. Meet with each informant individually and discuss the purpose of your visit, the concept of wealth and the word chosen for it. Discuss briefly the differences between rich and poor in the community.

5. Explain that you would like them to sort the cards into groups according to differences in wealth. The informant decides how many groups to have and may change this as the sorting progresses. It is sometimes easiest to start off with three groups – rich, medium and poor – and then sub-divide groups later if necessary. If the person is illiterate, read out the name on the card to them.

6. Read back the names in each pile to check they have made no mistakes. If any pile contains more than 40 per cent of households ask the informant to subdivide it again.

7. Discuss with the informant the characteristics of each group.

8. Write down the household numbers in each group on a recording sheet and make notes about the characteristics of each group.

9. Repeat this wealth ranking exercise with the other informants.

Stage 3: Calculating the wealth score for each household

10. From each informant's ranking exercise, calculate a score for each household based on the wealth group they were placed in. Each wealth group is numbered; the richest group is 1, the next richest is 2, and so on. The household's score is their wealth group number divided by the total number of groups, rounded to the nearest whole number.

$$\frac{\text{Wealth Group Number}}{\text{Total Number of Groups}} \times 100 = \textbf{Household Score}$$

$$\left(\frac{2}{4} \times 100 = 50 \right)$$

11. List the individual household scores for each informant in a table as shown below.

Household Number	Household Score For Each Informant			Average Score	Rank
	Informant				
	1	2	3		
1	67	50	50	55	15
2	.	.	.	.	.

12. Calculate the average ranking score for each household (total scores of each household divided by number of scores), that have been scored by at least two informants.

13. This average ranking score represents a false degree of accuracy, so households are usually divided into **wealth strata.** List the households in order from the lowest score (richest) to the highest score (poorest). Divide into groups of roughly equal size. The number of groups should be more than three and not more than the number of groups used by the informants.

APPENDIX 3

SELECTING CLUSTERS FOR A NUTRITION SURVEY

(Read the explanation of sampling, page 29 ff. before reading this Appendix.)

1. Decide on the population of interest

Is it the whole region or a particular area like a village or a camp? Remember, if you measure the rate of malnutrition in the whole region it will not show you differences within the region.

2. Divide the population into natural groupings

The groupings should have roughly the same characteristics. Where the total survey area is small and contained, as in a camp or large village, divide the area into sections of roughly equal population size. The number of sections equals the total number of clusters in the survey. A cluster of children are then chosen from each area to be weighed and measured.

In a larger area, such as a district or region, the obvious natural groupings are villages. If the area to be surveyed is very large, the number of villages will be much greater than the required number of clusters, in which case the clusters should be chosen from a list of all possible villages by 'assigning probability proportional to size'. This method of selecting children ensures that all children in the population have an equal chance of being selected, irrespective of whether they come from large or small villages.

3. Choose clusters by assigning probability proportional to size

Make a list of all villages with their individual populations and cumulative population. They can be listed in any order.

Village	Population (number of households)		Cumulative Total
A	345		345
B	235	235 + 345 =	580
C	189	189 + 580 =	769
D	398	398 + 769 =	807
E	453	453 + 807 =	1260
...	...	... + 1260 =	...
Total			15896

Villages or clusters are selected from this list at equal intervals (the sampling interval). To calculate the sampling interval, divide the total population by the number of clusters: 15896/30 = 412

The first cluster is selected by choosing a random number between 1 and 412 using random number tables. If the random number is 321 it corresponds to Village A as 321 lies between 0 and 345 of the cumulative total column. The others will be:

321   – Village A
321 + 412 =   733   – Village C
733 + 412 = 1145   – Village E ...

In this way 30 villages are selected at random. (If a village is above a certain size, it may be selected twice. This means that two clusters should be selected from that village.)

Make a rough sketch map of the village or area, making sure you know where the boundaries are. Go to the centre of the area. Choose a direction to walk in by spinning a pen, and walk in that direction counting the number of houses, tents or compounds you pass on either your left or your right until you reach the boundary.

Choose a number at random between one and the total number of huts passed. If the number is six, then the sixth house from the starting point is the first house you should visit to measure the children living there.

After that house, go to the next nearest house. Continue going to the next nearest house until you have found enough children for that cluster.

APPENDIX 4

NUTRITION SURVEY STATISTICS

1. Calculating the nutritional status of an individual

Percentage weight for height/length

$$\%WFH/L = \frac{\text{Actual weight}}{\text{Average weight of a child of the same height}} \times 100$$

For example, a child's height is 102cm and their weight is 15.4kg. From Table 9, page 95, the average weight of a child of 102cm is 16.1kg.

$$\%WFH/L = \frac{15.4}{16.1} \times 100 = 95.7\%$$

Z scores

Z scores are most easily explained by using an actual example. The graph in Figure 7 shows the weights of children of the same height; weight is along the bottom axis and the number of children on the left-hand axis. These children are girls who all measure 106cm tall and are from the NCHS/CDC/WHO reference population. Their average weight is 17.0kg. Half the children weigh more than average and half weigh less than average.

The standard deviation is a measure of **dispersion** (the spread of values) around the average weight of 17kg. In this example there are two standard deviations because the distribution curve is not symmetrical. The standard deviation for the left side of the curve is 1.5 and the standard deviation for the right side of the curve is 1.8.

The Z score expresses a child's weight as a **multiple** of the standard deviation of the reference population. For example, a girl weighing 15.5kg is 1.5kg or **one standard deviation below** the average weight of 17kg. This is expressed as having a Z score of -1.0.

To calculate Z scores:

$$Z \text{ Score} = \frac{\left[\begin{array}{c}\text{Weight of} \\ \text{individual child}\end{array}\right] - \left[\begin{array}{c}\text{Average weight of} \\ \text{children of same height*}\end{array}\right]}{\text{Standard Deviation of children of same height*}}$$

* From Reference Population shown in Table 9.

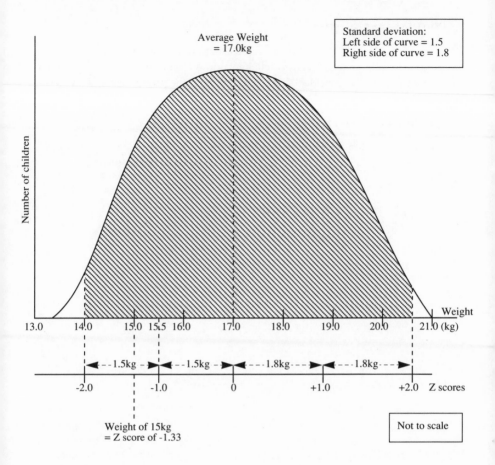

Figure 7: Weight distribution of girls whose height is 106cm.

For example, the Z score of a girl 106cm tall and weighing 15.0kg is:

$$\frac{15.0 - 17.0}{1.5} = -1.33$$

The weights of most children (95 per cent) are between plus two and minus two Z scores (shaded area on graph in Figure 7).

Z scores are usually only calculated when a computer and appropriate software is available to analyse the data. One reason for this is because plasticised cards showing tables of standard deviations for different heights are not available for use in the field.

2. Population statistics

The most useful nutrition survey statistics include the proportion of children malnourished and the mean nutritional status of the children in the sample, plus the standard error and confidence intervals for both the proportion and mean.

Proportion of children malnourished in the sample

The proportion is the number of children who are malnourished in relation to the total number of children in the sample and is calculated as shown:

$$\text{Proportion malnourished} = \left(\frac{\text{Total number of malnourished children}}{} \Big/ \frac{\text{Total number of children measured}}{} \right) \times 100$$

$$p = (y / n) \times 100$$

p : proportion malnourished
y : total number of malnourished children
n : total number of children measured

For example, if 300 children are measured (30 clusters of 10 children) and 65 children are found to be malnourished the proportion of malnutrition is:

$(65 / 300) \times 100 = 21.7\%$

The standard error of the proportion

The standard error is a measure of variation in the sample. The standard error allows the malnutrition rate in the population to be estimated. It is based on the differences between each cluster and the sample proportion.

There are two ways of calculating the standard error of the proportion; the easiest way is to use a calculator with a standard deviation function, but it is possible to do the calculation manually. The calculator method of calculating standard error is inexact and assumes that rates of malnutrition vary little between clusters (the proportion malnourished in the total sample is similar to the average of all the individual cluster proportions). If this seems to be true the calculator method is adequate. If this assumption is false, you must calculate the standard error manually.

i. Calculation of the standard error of a proportion using a statistical calculator

Calculate the proportion malnourished in each cluster and list in a table (Table 6).

Ensure the calculator is in standard deviation mode.

Clear the memory by pressing $\boxed{\text{INV}}$ and $\boxed{\text{AC}}$ together.

Enter the proportion malnourished in the first cluster using the number buttons.

Press the $\boxed{\text{M+}}$ button.

Enter the other cluster proportions in the same way.

Press the button marked $\boxed{\sigma_{n-1}}$ to show the standard deviation of the cluster proportions.

Divide this figure by the square root of the total number of clusters.

$$s = \frac{\sigma_{n-1}}{\sqrt{c}}$$

s : standard error

σ_{n-1}: standard deviation of the cluster proportions

c : number of clusters

For example, if the standard deviation of the cluster proportions is 13.44, the standard error will be:

$$s = \frac{13 \cdot 44}{\sqrt{30}} = 2 \cdot 45$$

ii. Calculation of the standard error manually

The standard error is calculated using a mathematical formula:

$$\text{Standard error of the proportion} = \sqrt{\left\{ \sum (p_i - p)^2 \Big/ \left(c \times (c-1) \right) \right\}}$$

p_i : proportion malnourished in cluster i

This may look complicated but is easy to calculate if taken step by step.

1 Cluster c_i	2 Number in each Cluster x_i	3 Number Malnourished y_i	4 Proportion Malnourished (column3/column2)×100 P_i	5 Difference (column 4-p) $(P_i - P)$	6 Difference squared (column 5)^2 $(P_i - P)^2$
1	10	2	20·00	−1·67	2·78
2	10	4	40·00	18·33	336·11
3	10	3	30·00	8·33	69·44
4	10	2	20·00	−1·67	2·78
5	10	3	30·00	8·33	69·44
6	10	1	10·00	−11·67	136·11
28	10	3	30·00	8·33	69·44
29	10	3	30·00	8·33	69·44
30	10	3	30·00	8·33	69·44
30 c	300 n	65 y	21·67 P		5416·67 $\sum(P - P_i)^2$

Table 6: Calculating the Standard Error of the Proportion from Cluster Survey Data

To calculate $\sum \left(P_i - P \right)^2$ make a table with six columns (Table 6).

From your survey results fill in the columns of the table as follows:

Column 1: The number of each cluster.

Column 2: The number of children in each cluster.

Column 3: The number of children malnourished in each cluster.

Column 4: The proportion malnourished in each cluster.

Column 5: Subtract the proportion malnourished in the total sample from the proportion malnourished in each cluster.

Column 6: Square the figure in Column 5 (multiply it by itself).

Add up the total for Column 6.

Now you can insert the appropriate figures into the formula and calculate the standard error.

In this example the standard error is:

$$s = \sqrt{\left\{ 5416 \cdot 67 \ \Big/ \ \big(30 \times (30-1)\big) \right\}}$$

$$= \sqrt{5416 \cdot 67 \ \Big/ \ 870}$$

$$= \sqrt{6 \cdot 226}$$

$$= 2 \cdot 49$$

The confidence interval for the proportion malnourished in the population

The confidence interval is a range of values between which you can be fairly certain the true rate of malnutrition in the population lies.

The confidence interval is the range between the sample proportion plus two and minus two standard errors.

Confidence interval $= p + (2 \times s)$ and $p - (2 \times s)$
of the proportion

In this example $= 21 \cdot 7 + (2 \times 2 \cdot 49)$ and $21 \cdot 7 - (2 \times 2 \cdot 49)$

So we can say with 95 per cent certainty that the rate of malnutrition in this population lies somewhere between 16.7 per cent and 26.7 per cent.

The mean nutrition status of the children in the sample

The mean (or average) is calculated by adding all the individual children's nutritional status (percentage weight for height) and dividing this by the total number of children.

$$\text{Mean} = \frac{\text{Sum of all childrens \%WFH}}{\text{Total number of children}}$$

$$x = 25561 \cdot 8 / 300 = 85 \cdot 2 \%$$

The standard error and confidence interval for the mean

This is calculated using the same formula as the standard error of the proportion, substituting the figure for mean %WFH for the figure for proportion malnourished:

$$\text{Standard error of the mean} = \sqrt{\left\{ \sum \left(x_i - x \right) \Big/ \left(c \times (c-1) \right) \right\}}$$

(The table for calculating $\sum \left(x_i - x \right)$ is Table 7.)

In this example, the standard error of the mean is:

$$s = \sqrt{152 \cdot 03 / \left(30 \times (30-1) \right)} = 0 \cdot 42$$

The confidence limits are —

$$85 \cdot 2 + (2 \times 0 \cdot 42) \quad \text{and} \quad 85 \cdot 2 - (2 \times 0 \cdot 42)$$

From this figure you can calculate the confidence interval for the mean. The average nutritional status in the population is therefore between 84.4 per cent and 86.0 per cent.

1 Clusters	2 Average nutritional status in each cluster	3 Difference (column2−x) $(x_i - x)$	4 Difference squared $(column3)^2$ $(x_i - x)^2$
1	84·77	−0·44	0·19
2	84·55	−0·66	0·43
3	85·47	0·26	0·07
4	85·55	0·34	0·12
5	86·44	1·23	1·52
6	84·31	−0·90	0·80
28	85·67	0·46	0·22
29	84·19	−1·02	1·03
30	84·92	−0·29	0·08
30	85·206		152·03
n	x		$\sum (x_i - x)^2$

Table 7: Calculating the Standard Error of the mean from Cluster Survey Data

APPENDIX 5

HOW TO MEASURE CHILDREN

Three people are needed to measure the weights and heights of children. The most experienced field worker (the measuring team leader) should position the child correctly and take the readings. The second most experienced person should record the measurements on the recording form. They should repeat the measurement out loud to check they heard it correctly. A third person assists the team leader to lift or position the child.

Be relaxed and friendly and reassure the children and their mothers. If one child begins to cry or becomes anxious, others will follow suit, and accurate measurements will be even more difficult to make.

Weighing and measuring is tiring. As people become tired, accuracy suffers. Ensure adequate rests and periodically double check measurements. Weighing and measuring is disruptive. If children are to be measured it is very difficult to ask mothers any more than the most simple questions. It is preferable to separate any weighing and measuring from interviews.

Measuring weight

● Use 25kg hanging Salter or CMS scales. They are strong, reliable and provide the necessary degree of precision.

● Use a piece of rope to secure the scales to a tree, or ceiling or from a strong pole supported on the shoulders of two people. The dial should be at eye level.

● Before each weighing session check scales with a standard weight (use a stone or jerrycan of sand that you have accurately measured beforehand). In case of inaccuracies, have a spare set of scales available.

● Adjust the needle to zero. If a heavy basket is used to suspend children, hang it on the scales when you adjust them to zero.

● Place small babies and infants in either hanging pants, a sling, or local basket, and attach to the scales. Older children are able to hold on to the bar attached to the scales and lift themselves off the ground.

● Ensure that nothing is touching the child. Stand directly in front of the dial and read the measurement to the nearest 0.1kg.

● Record the weight and any noticeable signs of malnutrition.

Measuring height and length

Height and length may be measured using the same board (Figure 8). Measure the height of children of 85cm and above, who are able to stand. Measure the length of children less than 85cm and those who are unable to stand. When the length of a child above 85cm is measured, 1cm should be subtracted from their length to give the equivalent height measurement.

Height

● Stand the child up straight on the base of the height board. The head, back and heels should be flat against the back of the board, with heels together and eyes looking straight ahead.

● Position the head block flat against the board and slide down on to the child's head. Ensure it is level (both tape measures should show the same readings).

● Read the height measurement to the nearest 0.5cm and call it out to the person recording the data.

Length

● Position the height/length board horizontally.

● Two people should lay the child on the board, with the child's head towards the base board. The assistant measurer holds the child's head against the base of the board, with the eyes looking straight up.

● The measuring team leader adjusts the measuring block and brings it to rest flat against the soles of the child's feet (one hand holds the block and the other holds the child's ankles).

● The team leader checks the block is level and reads the measurement to the nearest 0.5cm and calls it out to the person recording the data.

The construction of a height and length board

Use wood that is smooth and has no splinters or rough edges. The three blocks of wood on the base give it greater stability when used as a length board.

It is easier to read measurements from above the measuring block than beneath it. For this reason, position the ends of the tape measures 10cm from the base board (10cm being the height of the measuring block). This means that measurements may be read from above the block rather than beneath it.

Each board should always be used with the original block used to position the tapes. Label the board and block so they can be easily identified and always used together.

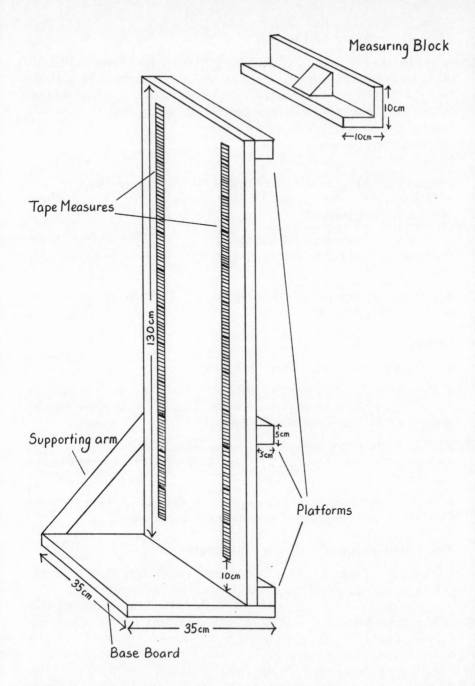

Measuring Block

Tape Measures

130 cm

Supporting arm

35 cm

10 cm

5 cm

5 cm

Platforms

10 cm

35 cm

Base Board

10 cm

10 cm

Figure 8: A height and length board

Table 8: Weight for length for boys and girls between 49 and 84.5cm

BOYS					**GIRLS**				

LENGTH CM	−3S.D.	−2S.D.	−1S.D.	MEDIAN	LENGTH CM	−3S.D.	−2S.D.	−1S.D.	MEDIAN
49.0	2.1	2.5	2.8	3.1	49.0	2.2	2.6	2.9	3.3
49.5	2.1	2.5	2.9	3.2	49.5	2.2	2.6	3.0	3.4
50.0	2.2	2.5	2.9	3.3	50.0	2.3	2.6	3.0	3.4
50.5	2.2	2.6	3.0	3.4	50.5	2.3	2.7	3.1	3.5
51.0	2.2	2.6	3.1	3.5	51.0	2.3	2.7	3.1	3.5
51.5	2.3	2.7	3.1	3.6	51.5	2.4	2.8	3.2	3.6
52.0	2.3	2.8	3.2	3.7	52.0	2.4	2.8	3.3	3.7
52.5	2.4	2.8	3.3	3.8	52.5	2.5	2.9	3.4	3.8
53.0	2.4	2.9	3.4	3.9	53.0	2.5	3.0	3.4	3.9
53.5	2.5	3.0	3.5	4.0	53.5	2.6	3.1	3.5	4.0
54.0	2.6	3.1	3.6	4.1	54.0	2.7	3.1	3.6	4.1
54.5	2.6	3.2	3.7	4.2	54.5	2.7	3.2	3.7	4.2
55.0	2.7	3.3	3.8	4.3	55.0	2.8	3.3	3.8	4.3
55.5	2.8	3.3	3.9	4.5	55.5	2.9	3.4	3.9	4.4
56.0	2.9	3.5	4.0	4.6	56.0	3.0	3.5	4.0	4.5
56.5	3.0	3.6	4.1	4.7	56.5	3.0	3.6	4.1	4.6
57.0	3.1	3.7	4.3	4.8	57.0	3.1	3.7	4.2	4.8
57.5	3.2	3.8	4.4	5.0	57.5	3.2	3.8	4.3	4.9
58.0	3.3	3.9	4.5	5.1	58.0	3.3	3.9	4.4	5.0
58.5	3.4	4.0	4.6	5.2	58.5	3.4	4.0	4.6	5.1
59.0	3.5	4.1	4.8	5.4	59.0	3.5	4.1	4.7	5.3
59.5	3.6	4.2	4.9	5.5	59.5	3.6	4.2	4.8	5.4
60.0	3.7	4.4	5.0	5.7	60.0	3.7	4.3	4.9	5.5
60.5	3.8	4.5	5.1	5.8	60.5	3.8	4.4	5.1	5.7
61.0	4.0	4.6	5.3	5.9	61.0	3.9	4.6	5.2	5.8
61.5	4.1	4.8	5.4	6.1	61.5	4.0	4.7	5.3	6.0
62.0	4.2	4.9	5.6	6.2	62.0	4.1	4.8	5.4	6.1
62.5	4.3	5.0	5.7	6.4	62.5	4.2	4.9	5.6	6.2
63.0	4.5	5.2	5.8	6.5	63.0	4.4	5.0	5.7	6.4
63.5	4.6	5.3	6.0	6.7	63.5	4.5	5.2	5.8	6.5
64.0	4.7	5.4	6.1	6.8	64.0	4.6	5.3	6.0	6.7
64.5	4.9	5.6	6.3	7.0	64.5	4.7	5.4	6.1	6.8
65.0	5.0	5.7	6.4	7.1	65.0	4.8	5.5	6.3	7.0
65.5	5.1	5.8	6.5	7.3	65.5	4.9	5.7	6.4	7.1
66.0	5.3	6.0	6.7	7.4	66.0	5.1	5.8	6.5	7.3
66.5	5.4	6.1	6.8	7.6	66.5	5.2	5.9	6.7	7.4
67.0	5.5	6.2	7.0	7.7	67.0	5.3	6.0	6.8	7.5
67.5	5.7	6.4	7.1	7.8	67.5	5.4	6.2	6.9	7.7
68.0	5.8	6.5	7.3	8.0	68.0	5.5	6.3	7.1	7.8
68.5	5.9	6.6	7.4	8.1	68.5	5.6	6.4	7.2	8.0
69.0	6.0	6.8	7.5	8.3	69.0	5.8	6.5	7.3	8.1
69.5	6.2	6.9	7.7	8.4	69.5	5.9	6.7	7.5	8.2

BOYS

LENGTH CM	−3S.D.	−2S.D.	−1S.D.	MEDIAN
70.0	6.3	7.0	7.8	8.5
70.5	6.4	7.2	7.9	8.7
71.0	6.5	7.3	8.1	8.8
71.5	6.7	7.4	8.2	8.9
72.0	6.8	7.5	8.3	9.1
72.5	6.9	7.7	8.4	9.2
73.0	7.0	7.8	8.6	9.3
73.5	7.1	7.9	8.7	9.5
74.0	7.2	8.0	8.8	9.6
74.5	7.3	8.1	8.9	9.7
75.0	7.4	8.2	9.0	9.8
75.5	7.5	8.3	9.1	9.9
76.0	7.6	8.4	9.2	10.0
76.5	7.7	8.5	9.3	10.2
77.0	7.8	8.6	9.4	10.3
77.5	7.9	8.7	9.5	10.4
78.0	8.0	8.8	9.7	10.5
78.5	8.1	8.9	9.8	10.6
79.0	8.2	9.0	9.9	10.7
79.5	8.2	9.1	10.0	10.8
80.0	8.3	9.2	10.1	10.9
80.5	8.4	9.3	10.1	11.0
81.0	8.5	9.4	10.2	11.1
81.5	8.6	9.5	10.3	11.2
82.0	8.7	9.6	10.4	11.3
82.5	8.8	9.6	10.5	11.4
83.0	8.8	9.7	10.6	11.5
83.5	8.9	9.8	10.7	11.6
84.0	9.0	9.9	10.8	11.7
84.5	9.1	10.0	10.9	11.8

GIRLS

LENGTH CM	−3S.D.	−2S.D.	−1S.D.	MEDIAN
70.0	6.0	6.8	7.6	8.4
70.5	6.1	6.9	7.7	8.5
71.0	6.2	7.0	7.8	8.6
71.5	6.3	7.1	8.0	8.8
72.0	6.4	7.2	8.1	8.9
72.5	6.5	7.4	8.2	9.0
73.0	6.6	7.5	8.3	9.1
73.5	6.7	7.6	8.4	9.3
74.0	6.8	7.7	8.5	9.4
74.5	6.9	7.8	8.6	9.5
75.0	7.0	7.9	8.7	9.6
75.5	7.1	8.0	8.8	9.7
76.0	7.2	8.1	8.9	9.8
76.5	7.3	8.2	9.0	9.9
77.0	7.4	8.3	9.1	10.0
77.5	7.5	8.4	9.2	10.1
78.0	7.6	8.5	9.3	10.2
78.5	7.7	8.6	9.4	10.3
79.0	7.8	8.7	9.5	10.4
79.5	7.9	8.7	9.6	10.5
80.0	8.0	8.8	9.7	10.6
80.5	8.0	8.9	9.8	10.7
81.0	8.1	9.0	9.9	10.8
81.5	8.2	9.1	10.0	10.9
82.0	8.3	9.2	10.1	11.0
82.5	8.4	9.3	10.2	11.1
83.0	8.5	9.4	10.3	11.2
83.5	8.6	9.5	10.4	11.3
84.0	8.7	9.6	10.5	11.4
84.5	8.7	9.6	10.6	11.5

(Source: NCHS/CDC/WHO Reference Population, from *Measuring Change in Nutritional Status*, 1983, WHO, Geneva)

Table 9: Weight for height for boys and girls between 85 and 130cm

STATURE CM	BOYS −3S.D.	−2S.D.	−1S.D.	MEDIAN	STATURE CM	GIRLS −3S.D.	−2S.D.	−1S.D.	MEDIAN
85.0	8.9	9.9	11.0	12.1	85.0	8.6	9.7	10.8	11.8
85.5	8.9	10.0	11.1	12.2	85.5	8.7	9.8	10.9	11.9
86.0	9.0	10.1	11.2	12.3	86.0	8.8	9.9	11.0	12.0
86.5	9.1	10.2	11.3	12.5	86.5	8.9	10.0	11.1	12.2
87.0	9.2	10.3	11.5	12.6	87.0	9.0	10.1	11.2	12.3
87.5	9.3	10.4	11.6	12.7	87.5	9.1	10.2	11.3	12.4
88.0	9.4	10.5	11.7	12.8	88.0	9.2	10.3	11.4	12.5
88.5	9.5	10.6	11.8	12.9	88.5	9.3	10.4	11.5	12.6
89.0	9.6	10.7	11.9	13.0	89.0	9.3	10.5	11.6	12.7
89.5	9.7	10.8	12.0	13.1	89.5	9.4	10.6	11.7	12.8
90.0	9.8	10.9	12.1	13.3	90.0	9.5	10.7	11.8	12.9
90.5	9.9	11.0	12.2	13.4	90.5	9.6	10.7	11.9	13.0
91.0	9.9	11.1	12.3	13.5	91.0	9.7	10.8	12.0	13.2
91.5	10.0	11.2	12.4	13.6	91.5	9.8	10.9	12.1	13.3
92.0	10.1	11.3	12.5	13.7	92.0	9.9	11.0	12.2	13.4
92.5	10.2	11.4	12.6	13.9	92.5	9.9	11.1	12.3	13.5
93.0	10.3	11.5	12.8	14.0	93.0	10.0	11.2	12.4	13.6
93.5	10.4	11.6	12.9	14.1	93.5	10.1	11.3	12.5	13.7
94.0	10.5	11.7	13.0	14.2	94.0	10.2	11.4	12.6	13.9
94.5	10.6	11.8	13.1	14.3	94.5	10.3	11.5	12.8	14.0
95.0	10.7	11.9	13.2	14.5	95.0	10.4	11.6	12.9	14.1
95.5	10.8	12.0	13.3	14.6	95.5	10.5	11.7	13.0	14.2
96.0	10.9	12.1	13.4	14.7	96.0	10.6	11.8	13.1	14.3
96.5	11.0	12.2	13.5	14.8	96.5	10.7	11.9	13.2	14.5
97.0	11.0	12.4	13.7	15.0	97.0	10.7	12.0	13.3	14.6
97.5	11.1	12.5	13.8	15.1	97.5	10.8	12.1	13.4	14.7
98.0	11.2	12.6	13.9	15.2	98.0	10.9	12.2	13.5	14.9
98.5	11.3	12.7	14.0	15.4	98.5	11.0	12.3	13.7	15.0
99.0	11.4	12.8	14.1	15.5	99.0	11.1	12.4	13.8	15.1
99.5	11.5	12.9	14.3	15.6	99.5	11.2	12.5	13.9	15.2
100.0	11.6	13.0	14.4	15.7	100.0	11.3	12.7	14.0	15.4
100.5	11.7	13.1	14.5	15.9	100.5	11.4	12.8	14.1	15.5
101.0	11.8	13.2	14.6	16.0	101.0	11.5	12.9	14.3	15.6
101.5	11.9	13.3	14.7	16.2	101.5	11.6	13.0	14.4	15.8
102.0	12.0	13.4	14.9	16.3	102.0	11.7	13.1	14.5	15.9
102.5	12.1	13.6	15.0	16.4	102.5	11.8	13.2	14.6	16.0
103.0	12.2	13.7	15.1	16.6	103.0	11.9	13.3	14.7	16.2
103.5	12.3	13.8	15.3	16.7	103.5	12.0	13.4	14.9	16.3
104.0	12.4	13.9	15.4	16.9	104.0	12.1	13.5	15.0	16.5
104.5	12.6	14.0	15.5	17.0	104.5	12.2	13.7	15.1	16.6
105.0	12.7	14.2	15.6	17.1	105.0	12.3	13.8	15.3	16.7
105.5	12.8	14.3	15.8	17.3	105.5	12.4	13.9	15.4	16.9

BOYS

STATURE CM	-3S.D.	-2S.D.	-1S.D.	MEDIAN
106.0	12.9	14.4	15.9	17.4
106.5	13.0	14.5	16.1	17.6
107.0	13.1	14.7	16.2	17.7
107.5	13.2	14.8	16.3	17.9
108.0	13.4	14.9	16.5	18.0
108.5	13.5	15.0	16.6	18.2
109.0	13.6	15.2	16.8	18.3
109.5	13.7	15.3	16.9	18.5
110.0	13.8	15.4	17.1	18.7
110.5	14.0	15.6	17.2	18.8
111.0	14.1	15.7	17.4	19.0
111.5	14.2	15.9	17.5	19.1
112.0	14.4	16.0	17.7	19.3
112.5	14.5	16.1	17.8	19.5
113.0	14.6	16.3	18.0	19.6
113.5	14.8	16.4	18.1	19.8
114.0	14.9	16.6	18.3	20.0
114.5	15.0	16.7	18.5	20.2
115.0	15.2	16.9	18.6	20.3
115.5	15.3	17.1	18.8	20.5
116.0	15.5	17.2	18.9	20.7
116.5	15.6	17.4	19.1	20.9
117.0	15.8	17.5	19.3	21.1
117.5	15.9	17.7	19.5	21.2
118.0	16.1	17.9	19.6	21.4
118.5	16.2	18.0	19.8	21.6
119.0	16.4	18.2	20.0	21.8
119.5	16.6	18.4	20.2	22.0
120.0	16.7	18.5	20.4	22.2
120.5	16.9	18.7	20.6	22.4
121.0	17.0	18.9	20.7	22.6
121.5	17.2	19.1	20.9	22.8
122.0	17.4	19.2	21.1	23.0
122.5	17.5	19.4	21.3	23.2
123.0	17.7	19.6	21.5	23.4
123.5	17.9	19.8	21.7	23.6
124.0	18.0	20.0	21.9	23.9
124.5	18.2	20.2	22.1	24.1
125.0	18.4	20.4	22.3	24.3
125.5	18.6	20.5	22.5	24.5
126.0	18.7	20.7	22.8	24.8
126.5	18.9	20.9	23.0	25.0

GIRLS

STATURE CM	-3S.D.	-2S.D.	-1S.D.	MEDIAN
106.0	12.5	14.0	15.5	17.0
106.5	12.6	14.1	15.7	17.2
107.0	12.7	14.3	15.8	17.3
107.5	12.8	14.4	15.9	17.5
108.0	13.0	14.5	16.1	17.6
108.5	13.1	14.6	16.2	17.8
109.0	13.2	14.8	16.4	17.9
109.5	13.3	14.9	16.5	18.1
110.0	13.4	15.0	16.6	18.2
110.5	13.6	15.2	16.8	18.4
111.0	13.7	15.3	16.9	18.6
111.5	13.8	15.5	17.1	18.7
112.0	14.0	15.6	17.2	18.9
112.5	14.1	15.7	17.4	19.0
113.0	14.2	15.9	17.5	19.2
113.5	14.4	16.0	17.7	19.4
114.0	14.5	16.2	17.9	19.5
114.5	14.6	16.3	18.0	19.7
115.0	14.8	16.5	18.2	19.9
115.5	14.9	16.6	18.4	20.1
116.0	15.0	16.8	18.5	20.3
116.5	15.2	16.9	18.7	20.4
117.0	15.3	17.1	18.9	20.6
117.5	15.5	17.3	19.0	20.8
118.0	15.6	17.4	19.2	21.0
118.5	15.8	17.6	19.4	21.2
119.0	15.9	17.7	19.6	21.4
119.5	16.1	17.9	19.8	21.6
120.0	16.2	18.1	20.0	21.8
120.5	16.4	18.3	20.1	22.0
121.0	16.5	18.4	20.3	22.2
121.5	16.7	18.6	20.5	22.5
122.0	16.8	18.8	20.7	22.7
122.5	17.0	19.0	20.9	22.9
123.0	17.1	19.1	21.1	23.1
123.5	17.3	19.3	21.3	23.4
124.0	17.4	19.5	21.6	23.6
124.5	17.6	19.7	21.8	23.9
125.0	17.8	19.9	22.0	24.1
125.5	17.9	20.1	22.2	24.3
126.0	18.1	20.2	22.4	24.6
126.5	18.2	20.4	22.7	24.9

	BOYS						**GIRLS**			
STATURE CM						STATURE CM				
	−3S.D.	−2S.D.	−1S.D.	MEDIAN			−3S.D.	−2S.D.	−1S.D.	MEDIAN
127.0	19.1	21.1	23.2	25.2		127.0	18.4	20.6	22.9	25.1
127.5	19.2	21.3	23.4	25.5		127.5	18.6	20.8	23.1	25.4
128.0	19.4	21.5	23.6	25.7		128.0	18.7	21.0	23.3	25.7
128.5	19.6	21.7	23.8	26.0		128.5	18.9	21.2	23.6	25.9
129.0	19.8	21.9	24.1	26.2		129.0	19.0	21.4	23.8	26.2
129.5	19.9	22.1	24.3	26.5		129.5	19.2	21.6	24.1	26.5
130.0	20.1	22.3	24.5	26.8		130.0	19.4	21.8	24.3	26.8

(Source: NCHS/CDC/WHO Reference Population, from *Measuring Change in Nutritional Status,* 1983, WHO, Geneva)

Measuring mid-upper arm circumference (MUAC)

● Only measure MUAC on children between one and five years old. A one-year-old is normally above 75cm tall, can stand or walk, and has six teeth or more.

● Use a MUAC insertion tape to measure arm circumference. The thin end slips through the opening at the wider end and the measurement is read at the point indicated by the arrows.

● Measure MUAC on the left arm.

● To find the mid-point, stand the child facing you and ask the child to bend the left arm at the elbow at a right angle and place the left hand flat on the stomach. Use the MUAC tape to measure from the tip of the shoulder to the tip of the elbow.

● Take hold of the point of the tape at the elbow and fold backon to the point on the shoulder tip. Mark with a pen the position of the fold, which is the middle point of the upper arm.

● At the mid-point, wrap the tape closely round the arm. Do not pull tightly or leave loose. Read the measurement to the nearest 0.1cm.

Figure 9: An insertion tape

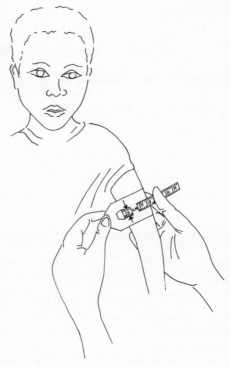

Figure 10: Using an insertion tape

NB If an insertion tape is unavailable, it is perfectly possible to use an ordinary tape measure; but in this case, it is best to start the measurement at the 10cm point, which will give you the first 10cm of the tape to hold.

APPENDIX 6

REPORT FORMAT

Title page: Title (location and date of visit), authors, team members, date of report and organisations involved. Brief purpose.

Contents: Section headings with heading numbers and page numbers.

Acknowledgements: Communities, advisers, team members, funders.

Summary and recommendations: This is a short version of the report to remind readers of the main points. Write it last.

Most of the summary should be conclusions and recommendations. Present recommendations in a list. Include a statement of costs, resources required, timing and other important details.

Introduction: Background information, aims of the assessment.

Methods: Details of methods, sampling methods, rapid assessment techniques, measuring techniques, nutrition indices, reasons for choice of villages and people interviewed.

Results: Summarise findings under headings. Where possible use maps, tables and diagrams.

Discussion: This may be combined with the results, rather than being a separate section. Discuss the implications of your findings:

How severe are the problems?

How are people coping?

How can the agency support them?

What are the logistical problems?

What are the future prospects?

Conclusions: Conclusions present a summing up of the answers to the original questions, without repeating facts presented in the results and discussion, and the action proposed.

APPENDIX 7

VITAMIN AND MINERAL DEFICIENCIES

Vitamin and mineral deficiencies are caused by a lack of essential minerals or vitamins in the diet. They may cause permanent damage to health and even death.

In times of food scarcity and famine, the most important deficiency disease is xerophthalmia – vitamin A deficiency – which can cause permanent blindness and may also contribute to increased incidence, severity and duration of infectious diseases such as measles, diarrhoea and respiratory tract infections.

Where people are totally dependent on food aid rations, other deficiency diseases may also develop, for example, scurvy (vitamin C deficiency), pellagra (niacin deficiency) or nutritional anaemias (iron or folic acid deficiency).

To assess if vitamin deficiencies might be a problem look for the danger signs listed below:

● Total dependence on food rations which are low in essential vitamins and minerals.

● A previous period of hardship: failed harvest, which means a prolonged hungry season; travelling for several weeks; destitution and limited access to food.

● A switch from lightly milled local cereals or a diet based on animal products, to highly refined cereals, such as white flour or polished rice.

● A lack of green leafy vegetables, unmilled cereals and dried peas and beans in local markets.

● A maize-based diet low in protein.

● Evidence of protein energy malnutrition.

Actions to treat and prevent vitamin deficiencies should be taken if any of these danger signs exist. Do not wait until a proper survey to estimate the prevalence of vitamin deficiencies is completed.

IF THE FIRST TWO DANGER SIGNS ARE PRESENT, DISTRIBUTE VITAMIN A TO ALL CHILDREN AGED FIVE AND BELOW. Vitamin A deficiency can be prevented by a one-off distribution of vitamin A capsules every six months. It is not possible to give similar protection against other deficiencies, because the other vitamins are not stored in the body and must be consumed on a daily basis.

Distribution of vitamin pills on a regular basis to a large population is impractical; it is logistically difficult, culturally inappropriate and requires vast quantities of pills and a well established distribution network. Instead, consider the following options for prevention:

● Distribute foods containing the essential nutrients.

● Distribute a larger ration to allow trading in local markets for more nutritious foods.

● Distribute fortified foods to the most vulnerable groups, such as fortified biscuits; fortified dried skimmed milk as part of a porridge pre-mix or prepared under supervision; or fortified cereal-legume pre-mixes (Corn Soy Milk).

● Support home and communal gardens by providing tools and seeds and supporting demonstration plots.

Vitamin A deficiency – xeropthalmia

If not recognised and treated, vitamin A deficiency can lead to permanent blindness. Measles may be more severe and of longer duration among children with vitamin A deficiency and is associated with a higher risk of mortality. Measles contributes to post-illness malnutrition and will rapidly deplete stores of vitamin A. Treatment with high doses of vitamin A is therefore vital. The most important target groups are those who show signs of deficiency, those with infectious diseases, and those suffering from malnutrition.

Communities affected by food scarcity and famine are at risk of developing vitamin A deficiency. In these situations prevention of vitamin A deficiency is essential. Large doses of vitamin A should be administered to all children under six years old. Supplementation doses of vitamin A to prevent deficiency are as follows:

Children over 1 year and under 6 years	200,000 IU orally every 3 to 6 months
Infants 6 – 12 months and older children who weigh less than 8 kg.	100,000 IU orally every 3 to 6 months
Lactating mothers	200,000 IU orally once at delivery or during the next 2 months.

200,000 IU = 60,000mg retinol

There are two main forms of vitamin A: retinol (preformed vitamin A), and beta carotene (an orange or red pigment found in fruits and vegetables), which the human body converts to vitamin A. The biological activity of vitamin A is expressed as Retinol Equivalents (RE):

1 RE = 1 µg retinol or 6 µg beta carotene.

The biological activity of vitamin A may also be expressed as International Units (IU); 1 I.U. = 0.3 µg retinol.

Daily requirements: (FAO/WHO recommended requirements)

	Retinol equivalents µg/day
Infants	350
Pregnant women	600
Lactating women	850

Supplementation: Supplementation with 200,000 IU vitamin A will give protection for from 3 to 6 months.

Food sources: Green leafy vegetables, deep yellow or orange fruits and vegetables, red palm oil, fortified margarine, whole milk, liver, dairy products. Fortified dried skimmed milk (1500 µg per 100 g dry weight). Corn soy milk (500 µg per 100 g dry weight).

Lead time: Vitamin A is stored in the liver and there may be a delay of several months before signs of deficiency show.

Signs and symptoms of deficiency:
Night blindness – unable to see in poor light (after sunset, inside huts), while those with normal sight are able to see well. Mothers may know that the night vision of their child is poor.
Conjunctival xerosis – Areas on the surface of the eyeball (conjunctive) become dry and dull.
Bitots spots – Foamy patches at the sides of the eye.
Corneal xerosis and ulceration – The central transparent part of the eye (cornea) becomes cloudy, followed by ulceration.
Keratomalacia – The cornea may burst leading, to loss of the eye contents and blindness.

Treatment of xerophthalmia:
Adult males, and children over 1 year: On diagnosis 200,000 IU vitamin A orally. The following day 200,000 IU vitamin A orally. Four weeks later 200,000 IU vitamin A orally.

Children under 1 year and children of any age who weigh less than 8kg:
Treat with half doses shown above.

Women of reproductive age, pregnant or not: For night blindness or Bitots spots treat with a daily dose of 10,000 IU daily for 2 weeks.

Vitamin C deficiency – scurvy

Refugees in camps in Somalia and Ethiopia and displaced people in Sudan have suffered from scurvy as a result of dependency on food rations low in vitamin C.

Daily requirements: 10 – 35mg daily in diet e.g. small tomato or leafy vegetable.

Food sources: Fresh fruits and vegetables, breast milk.

Lead time: Between 2–3 months.

Signs and symptoms: Scurvy is recognised by swollen and bleeding gums leading to loss of teeth and/or swollen, painful joints (in particular the hips and knees) that reduce mobility. Internal haemorrhaging can lead to death. Risk of mortality among pregnant women giving birth is greater if they are deficient in vitamin C.

Treatment: 300mg or more daily until recovery. A diet with plenty of fresh fruit and vegetables.

Thiamine deficiency – beriberi

This occurs where people have to exist on a starchy staple food such as cassava, or highly refined cereals like white polished rice. It has been found among refugees dependent on food rations.

Daily requirements: 1mg thiamine daily in diet (0.4mg per 1000Kcal).

Food sources: Dried peas and beans, whole grain or lightly milled cereals, groundnuts, oilseeds. Destroyed by cooking.

Lead time: 12 weeks.

Signs and symptoms: Several forms exist:
Moderate deficiency – loss of appetite, malaise and weakness, especially in the legs. This may last several months.
Dry beriberi – which may lead to paralysis of the limbs.
Wet beriberi – swelling of the body (oedema) and heart failure in infants, may cause sudden death.

Treatment: 50mg thiamine followed by 10mg daily until recovery.

Niacin deficiency – pellagra

Pellagra is endemic where people eat a maize based diet with little protein rich food. It is not associated with times of food scarcity and famine, although major outbreaks have occurred recently among refugees in Zimbabwe and Malawi.

Daily intake: 15 – 20mg niacin (6.6mg per 1,000Kcal). The niacin in maize is not all biologically available.

Food sources: Whole grain cereals, groundnuts, dried peas and beans, milk. Niacin is destroyed by long cooking.

Lead time: 2 to 3 months.

Signs and symptoms: It is characterised by a skin rash on those parts of the body exposed to sunlight (dermatitis). It can cause diarrhoea and dementia.

Treatment: 50 – 100mg of niacin orally daily until skin lesions recover (usually only a few days).

Anaemia

Anaemia is a low level of haemoglobin in the blood, which affects a person's ability to make sustained physical effort. Common symptoms are general fatigue, breathlessness and giddiness. The main causes are parasitic infections (particularly hookworm); low intake or poor absorption of iron and folic acid; the need to produce new blood cells (recovery from malnutrition, or malaria). Anaemia is common among women and children, particularly women who are pregnant or recently delivered.

Daily intake: Iron 10 – 28mg; Folic acid 170 – 200μg. Pregnant and lactating women should be given supplements from the fourth month of pregnancy; 120mg iron, and 0.2mg folic acid per day until the birth.

Food sources: Iron: dark green leaves, meat. Diets lacking in vitamin C and/or high in fibre reduce iron absorption.
Folic acid: dark green leafy vegetables, liver and kidney. Folic acid is destroyed by prolonged cooking.

Signs and symptoms: The tongue, finger nails or inside of the lower eyelid appear very pale. Children with severe anaemia are tired and listless and have a rapid pulse. Malnourished people are often anaemic.

Treatment: Adults: 200 – 250mg of ferrous sulphate in tablet form three times a day for at least 2 months. Children: 50mg ferrous sulphate mixture (liquid) diluted with water per day for each year of age. Treat any non-dietary causes of anaemia, such as hookworm or bleeding.

Iodine deficiency – goitre and cretinism

Iodine deficiency causes enlargement of the thyroid gland (goitre) and reproductive failure. Children born to women deficient in iodine may suffer greater or lesser degrees of mental impairment (cretinism). Goitre is rarely seen in young children.

Simple goitre, where the gland is just visible and palpable, are found in all parts of the world but do not usually affect health. Iodine deficiency is most severe in poor, isolated inland communities where the soil is deficient in iodine. Some foods, for example, cabbages (brassica) and cassava, contain goitrogenic substances which interfere with the availability of iodine to the thyroid gland.

A relief programme may provide an opportunity to raise the problem of goitre as an issue to be dealt with, even though its direct cause was not due to the immediate problem of food scarcity and famine.

Daily intake: 100 – 150µg daily. 2ml iodised oil (475mg/ml)given orally is sufficient for up to 2 years.

Food source: Animal products, marine fish. Where the soil lacks iodine, the food grown will be deficient in iodine.

Treatment: A simple goitre rarely requires treatment. In time, with a good diet or with a diet supplemented with iodine, it will become smaller.

(For more details, see *Controlling Iodine Deficiency Disorders in Developing Countries: Oxfam Practical Health Guide 5.*)

APPENDIX 8

APPROXIMATE NUTRITIONAL VALUE OF FOOD AID COMMODITIES AND COMMON FOODS IN AFRICA

Food	Energy Kcal	Protein g	Fat g
Cereals			
Maize, white, meal	360	9.0	3.8
Millet, whole grain	315	7.4	1.3
Millet, flour	320	5.6	1.4
Rice, polished	360	7.0	0.5
Sorghum, whole grain	335	11.0	3.0
Sorghum, flour	335	9.5	2.8
Teff, whole grain	341	9.8	2.5
Wheat, whole grain	330	12.3	1.5
Wheat, flour	350	11.5	2.0
Beans, peas and lentils			
Beans, dried	335	22.0	1.5
Horse bean	342	25.0	1.5
Lentils, dried	325	25.0	1.2
Peas, dried	300	22.0	1.1
Soya beans	405	34.0	1.8
Nuts			
Groundnuts, fresh	345	19.0	6.2
Groundnuts, dried	570	23.0	45.0
Sugar	400		
Vegetable oil	900		100.0
Dried skimmed milk (DSM)	360	36.0	
Dried whole milk	490	23.5	24.0
Corn soy milk	380	18.0	6.0
Instant corn soy milk	365	12.2	4.0
Wheat soy blend	370	20.0	6.0
Oxfam food aid biscuits	465	8.6	18.0
Dried salted fish	270	47.0	7.5
Canned fish in oil	305	22.0	24.0
Dried fruit	270	4.0	0.5
Dried dates	245	2.0	0.5

APPENDIX 9

OXFAM KITS

There are several different Oxfam Kits for use in emergencies when time is short. They include both equipment and guidance. The kits are designed to allow a relief team to start work as soon as they arrive in the field. Most of the equipment in the kits could be bought in 'normal times', and the use of local resources is preferable where they are available and time is not a constraint. The Practical Guides included with the kits are available separately and are widely used by other agencies.

Kits for nutritional surveillance and feeding

These kits are designed for use in emergencies where large numbers of people are destitute and gathered in one place, such as a refugee situation or famine. In times of food scarcity they are less useful.

    The feeding kits do not contain food and are not designed to feed the whole community. The use of the kits presumes that people either have their own supplies of food or are receiving food from a general feeding programme.

Supplementary Feeding Kit

This is designed for the supplementary feeding of children and other people whose nutritional state is poor. The Kit caters for 250 people and besides feeding and cooking equipment, includes items for simple nutritional screening and monitoring. Stoves and other sources of heat for cooking are not included as conditions vary from one situation to another.

Ref No: OFK 2 – for 250 children
         OFK 5 – for 500 children

Therapeutic Feeding Kit

This is designed to provide therapeutic feeding for 100 severely malnourished children (below 70 per cent 'weight for height'). This kit is intended for rehabilitation and will not be used as often as the supplementary feeding kits. The therapeutic kit can be used by trained staff who are able to recognise and respond to the main health problems associated with severe malnutrition e.g. diarrhoea, dehydration and infections. Supervision of a therapeutic feeding programme needs to be by a suitably experienced person. Basic drugs and medical supplies are not included as they are usually available though the government system or relief supplies.

Ref No: OFK 3 – for 100 children

Nutrition Surveillance Equipment

This includes items for nutritional screening and monitoring of children and can be used in conjunction with the Feeding Kits (see below).
Ref No: OFK 1 – for 250 children

Mini Survey Kit

This is designed to help relief workers measure the nutritional status of children immediately on arrival. The kit fits into a small rucksack and includes a 25kg hanging scale and pants, tape measures, calculator, pens, pencils, stationery and weight for height tables.
Ref No: OFK 4

The emergency immunisation kit

This kit contains all the equipment necessary to immunise up to 5,000 people in an emergency with minimal back-up and support. The kit includes refrigerator, freezer, petrol driven generator and spares, 5,000 re-usable syringes and needles, immunisation cards and plastic wallet holders, rope, sheeting, registration books and administration material. All that needs to be added are vaccine and power (240 volts, 12 volts or fuel for the generator).

The Oxfam/Delagua water testing kit

This kit enables several important water quality tests to be undertaken in the field with little or no laboratory support. The kit can be used for continuous surveillance of water quality at points-of-use, water storage tanks and in treatment plants. The kit enables tests to be done for faecal coliform bacteria, free and total chlorine, pH, turbidity, temperature and conductivity. The use of the kit requires some training.

Supplied with the kit are materials sufficient for 200 faecal coliform tests; extra materials can be purchased separately.

APPENDIX 10

FOOD AID BISCUITS

Biscuits are a luxury item for most people and not a regular part of the diet. Most biscuits are expensive and are not a good source of nutrition. For these reasons the distribution of biscuits is inappropriate except in certain circumstances.

Oxfam have developed a special biscuit for use in times of famine and other emergencies. This biscuit is unlike many other biscuits, as it is a good source of nutrients and is packaged to withstand damage caused by rough handling during transport and poor storage conditions.

Oxfam biscuits are high in energy and rich in protein. One packet of six biscuits contains 520Kcal and 9.6g protein and at least half of the WHO/FAO recommended daily intakes of certain vitamins and minerals (those marked * below). They are semi-sweet, but otherwise plain and taste like any baked biscuit you might find in an African bakery.

Vitamin A (retinol)*	2500IU	Iron *	13.5mg
Vitamin B1 (thiamin)*	0.6mg	Iodine *	140µg
Vitamin B2 (riboflavin)*	0.9mg	Calcium *	600mg
Vitamin B6	0.9	Phosphorus	480mg
Vitamin B12 *	1.5µg	Sodium	200mg
Vitamin D *	200IU	Potassium	70mg
Nicotinamide	1.15mg		
Folic acid *	200µg		

Table 10: The vitamin and mineral content of Oxfam food aid biscuits

Packing: One packet of six biscuits weighs 112g. An airtight tin holds 90 packets.(Gross Weight 11.6kg; Net Weight 10kg; Size 240 x 240 x 380mm.) Shelf-life of two years.

The use of biscuits in an emergency

Food Aid biscuits provide instant energy and other nutrients. Unlike other foods that might be available, biscuits need no cooking and no careful measuring or preparation before eating. In the early stages of a sudden emergency, when people are without food or the equipment and fuel for its preparation, the distribution of biscuits provides immediate nourishment and can make all the difference to people's morale, and gives them confidence that help is being organised.

The biscuits main functions are for short-term supplementary feeding, until other alternatives can be established (for example, one biscuit ration i.e. one packet of six biscuits, plus high energy milk), and as part of a therapeutic feeding programme. Severely malnourished children often lose their appetite but may be coaxed to eat again by having a biscuit to suck. Biscuits are sometimes useful for the night feed, as fewer staff are available for preparation of food or supervision of feeding.

In 1985 in Sudan and Ethiopia, many hundreds of tons of Oxfam Food Aid Biscuits were used in feeding programmes. Relief workers had no doubts about their usefulness during the emergency, but realised that the use of biscuits had to be carefully controlled and supervised in special programmes.

It must be emphasised that very few biscuits are appropriate for use in emergencies. Oxfam Food Aid Biscuits have been carefully designed for use in emergencies related to food shortages. Further advice about the use of biscuits is given in the information leaflets enclosed with all packs of Oxfam Food Aid Biscuits.

APPENDIX 11

RECIPES FOR SUPPLEMENTARY FEEDING PROGRAMMES

Wherever possible, base your recipes on locally available foods, such as the local cereal, peas, beans or lentils and oil. Local foods may be used to show how to prepare nutritious weaning foods that cause malnourished children to gain weight. Imported foods may encourage people to think that imported foods are 'better'.

The amount of energy, protein and fat in the following recipes was calculated using the table in Appendix 8: The nutrient content of some common foods. The recipes given below meet the recommendations in Section 4.3 about the nutritional composition of foods used as food supplements: above 20 per cent of total energy from fat and about 12 per cent of total energy from protein.

Quantities of ingredients in the recipes are given in weights, which are more accurate than using volumes. However, scales are not always available and so volume measures must be used.

Dried milk powder	650g – 750g
Dried milk powder (granules)	350g – 400g
Millet, Rice, Wheat grain, Sorghum	710g – 860g
Wheat flour	550g – 600g
Bean flour	850g
Chickpeas, split peas, kidney beans, lentils	800g – 900g
Groundnuts, soya beans, butter beans	700g – 800g
Oil	900g – 950g
Sugar	900g – 950g

Table 11: The approximate weight of one litre volume of foods

Label all containers used for measuring volumes so they are used correctly. The volume of some ingredients, such as dried milk powder, varies with different brands. Always check new ingredients to see if their weight volume ratio differs.

Malted grain

Porridge made with flour from malted grain is more **energy dense** than porridge made with ordinary flour. This is because flour from malted grain does not thicken as much when cooked and so less water is needed to make a porridge of the same thickness. Malted grain has been dampened to allow it to germinate, then sun dried and milled into flour. This is a common practice in Africa.

Important rules

● Only use **safe water** – safe, piped water or water that has either been boiled and cooled or has been adequately chlorinated.

● Keep to the recipes – if you change them, make sure that fat still provides more than 20 per cent of total energy and protein about 12 per cent total energy.

● The calculation of the amount needed in the recipes is based on servings of 300mls of ready to eat food, which is all most small children are able to eat at one time.

● Keep the kitchen area clean and tidy and teach basic hygiene to the staff.

● The storage life of pre-mix is two weeks if kept in a clean, covered container. Prepared milk and porridge should never be kept longer than a few hours.

RECIPE 1: Porridge based on local ingredients

	Weight g	Energy Kcal	Protein g	Fat g
Sorghum flour	400	1340	44	12
Bean flour	200	670	44	3
Oil	100	900	-	100
Onion	50	19	-	-
Total weight	750	2929	88	115
Composition of 100g	100	390	12	15
Per cent of total energy:			12%	35%

To calculate quantities:

Quantity	6L	15L
Number of 300ml servings	20	50
Sorghum flour	860g	2.2kg
Bean flour	430g	1.1kg
Onion	60g	0.3kg
Oil	115g	0.55kg
Water	4.5L	11.2L

(one part of porridge mix to approximately 3 parts water)

Preparation: The bean flour is made from dried beans ground to a fine powder. Mix the bean flour to a smooth paste with some of the **safe** cold water. Add some more water. Bring to the boil and cook gently with the chopped onion. When nearly cooked, add the sorghum flour and stir well until cooked. Stir in the oil. The amount of water needed depends on how much the beans and flour will absorb.

(This recipe has been adapted from the recipes in: Cameron, M. and Hofvander, Y. (1983), *Manual on Feeding Infants and Young Children*, Oxford: Oxford University Press. This book contains numerous recipes based on locally available ingredients. The next three recipes are based on those found in: *Selective Feeding, Oxfam Practical Health Guide 1* and have all been successfully used in feeding programmes.)

RECIPE 2: Porridge based on a locally available flour and dried skimmed milk (DSM)

	Weight g	Energy Kcal	Protein g	Fat g
Pre-mix				
Maize flour	500	1800	45	19
Sugar	125	500	-	-
Dried skimmed milk	250	900	90	-
Oil	200	1800	-	200
Total weight	1075	5000	140	219
Composition of 100g	100	465	13	20
Percent of total energy:			11%	39%

To calculate quantities:

Amount of prepared porridge	3L	15L
Number of 300ml servings	10	50
Amount of pre-mix	750g	3.75kg
Maize flour	350g	1.75kg
Sugar	90g	0.44kg
DSM	175g	0.87kg
Oil	140g	0.70kg
Water	2.25L	11.25L

(one part pre-mix to three parts water)

To prepare pre-mix: Stir dry ingredients together until well mixed through.

To prepare porridge from pre-mix: Add enough **safe** cold water to the pre-mix to mix to a smooth paste. Gradually stir in the rest of the water. Bring to the boil and stir continuously until it is smooth and thick. Where large quantities are prepared the porridge may burn on the bottom of the pan. To prevent this bring the water to the boil before adding the water-pre-mix paste and stir until it is smooth and thick.

RECIPE 3: Porridge based on Corn Soya Milk (CSM)

	Weight	Energy	Protein	Fat
	g	Kcal	g	g
Pre-mix				
Corn Soya Milk	550	2090	99	33
Sugar	100	400	-	-
Oil	100	900	-	100
Total weight	750	3390	99	133
Composition of 100g	100	452	13	18
Per cent of total energy:			12%	35%

To calculate quantities:

Quantity of prepared porridge	3L	18L
Number of 300ml servings	10	60
Amount of pre-mix	750g	4.5kg
Corn Soya Milk	550g	3.3kg
Sugar	100g	0.6kg
Oil	100g	0.6kg
Water	2.25L	13.5L

(One part pre-mix to three parts water)

Prepare as for recipe 2.

Corn Soya Milk (CSM) is a blend of cereal flour, beans and DSM and fortified with vitamins and minerals. CSM is an American food aid commodity. Other cereal legume porridge mixes may be substituted for CSM. For example *faffa* is a similar porridge mix produced in Ethiopia.

RECIPE 4: High energy milk

	Weight g	Energy Kcal	Protein g	Fat g
Pre-mix				
Sugar	250	1000	-	-
Dried skimmed milk	420	1512	151	-
Oil	320	2880	-	320
Total weight	990	5392	151	320
Composition of 100g	100	545	15	32
Per cent of total energy:			11%	53%

To calculate quantities:

Quantity of prepared milk	6L	15L
Number of 300ml servings	20	50
Amount of pre-mix	1.2kg	3kg
Dried skimmed milk	510g	1.3kg
Sugar	300g	0.8kg
Oil	390g	1.0kg
Water	4.8L	12L

(one part pre-mix plus four parts water)

Prepare as for Recipe 2.

High energy milk should only be prepared under the strictest supervision with particular attention to hygiene, as it is an ideal medium for bacteria to grow in. Discard any left over milk or porridge and **never** keep it over night. High energy milk is an excellent food for treatment of malnourished children. **Do not reduce the amount of oil.**

APPENDIX 12

FOOD STORAGE

Outside stacking

Outside stacking of sacks of cereal grains covered with tarpaulins may control losses due to spoilage for three to six months, if properly arranged and managed.

Stacks should be built on either wooden pallets, sawn timber or beams, or on raised concrete plinths. This should prevent dampness in the ground seeping into the grain and will also reduce access for insects, but will not stop rodents. Keep the area around the stack tidy and clean so as not to attract rodents.

The tops of the sacks should be formed into a ridge and covered with tarpaulin secured in place with weights. The ridge allows rain water to run off.

Space for storage

One metric tonne of wheat is contained in twenty 50kg sacks and occupies 2 cubic metres when stacked ten sacks high. Wheat flour, porridge mixes and DSM take up more space than beans, sugar, rice and wheat grain.

Storage volume per metric tonne

Beans, rice, sugar, wheat grain   1.4 – 1.6 cubic metres
· Wheat flour, porridge mixes   2.0 – 2.2 cubic metres

Calculation of storage capacity

The usable space for a small store holding less than 500MT may be less than 50 per cent of the total space available, allowing for the space required around stacks and for passageways. The usable space increases with store size to around 70 to 80 per cent for stores holding 5,000 to 10,000MT.

Total volume of store = height x width x length
$$= 4 \times 12 \times 30 = 1440 \text{ cubic metres}$$

Total storage capacity of store
$$= (\text{total volume} / \text{storage volume of food}) \times \text{usable space}$$
$$= (1440 / 2.1) \times 0.5 = 343\text{MT wheat flour}$$

Food spoilage

If stored incorrectly, food may become damaged by moisture, rain, fungal or mould growth, or by pests (weevils, rats, mice, birds).

Mouldy Food: Remove any mould-damaged food to a depth of at least 3 to 4cm beyond the visible mould damage. If mould is present throughout the food, the food should be destroyed. Destroy groundnuts with obvious mould growth because of the risk of toxins.

Insects: A single consignment of cereals may be reduced by as much as 30 per cent in weight if attacked by insects whilst in storage. Insects eat the most nourishing part of the grain (the germ), which greatly reduces the amount of protein and vitamins present. Weevils are an exception as they prefer the starchy part of the grain. Any pest-damaged cereals are nutritionally inferior to good quality cereals, although it is not possible to measure the nutritional losses in the field. There is no rule for the permitted number of insects in cereals. The infested grain may still be eaten but has to be carefully sifted to remove insects and is unpalatable. Local food tastes should be respected.

Most insects do not thrive or are killed above 38°C and are killed below 0°C. Therefore, high or low temperatures may prevent the problem getting any worse. Small amounts of grain may be exposed to the sun for a few hours to reduce insect numbers.

Caking of DSM or other powdered products: If DSM becomes damp it will set solid. Severely caked powder should be used for animal feeding only. Moderately caked powder may be used by sieving out the caked portion.

Good storage practices

● Keep the stores clean and tidy; remove all food debris that might attract insects, birds, rats and mice.

● Separate any damaged or spoiled food; re-bag any food from damaged packaging that is still edible.

● Keep good storage records; use food in correct stock rotation (first in, first out).

● Make regular inspections; assess the quality of the food received for pest damage, condition of sacks etc, and regularly check its condition while it is in the stores.

FURTHER READING

Casley, D. J. and Lury, D. A. (1986), *Data Collection in Developing Countries*, Oxford: Clarendon Press.

Dreze, J. and Sen, A. (1989), *Hunger and Public Action*, Oxford: Clarendon Press.

Eade, D. and Williams, S. (eds), *Oxfam Manual for Development Workers* (formerly *Oxfam Field Director's Handbook*), New edition in preparation. Oxford: Oxfam.

Grandin, B.E.(1988), *Wealth Ranking in Smallholder Communities: a field manual*, London: Intermediate Technology Publications.

Howard, J. and Spice, R. (1989), *Plastic Sheeting: its use for emergency shelter and other purposes*, An Oxfam Technical Guide, Oxford: Oxfam.

Lusty, T. and Diskett, P. (1984), *Selective Feeding Programmes, Oxfam Practical Health Guide 1*, Oxford: Oxfam.

McCracken, J.A., Pretty, J. and Conway, G.R. (1988), *An Introduction to Rapid Rural Appraisal for Agricultural Development*, London: International Institute for Environment and Development.

— (1983), *Measuring Change in Nutritional Status: guidelines for assessing the nutritional impact of supplementary feeding programmes for vulnerable groups*, Geneva: WHO.

Mitchell, J. and Slim, H. (1991), *Registration in Emergencies, Oxfam Practical Health Guide 6*, Oxford: Oxfam.

Moser, C. and Kalton, G. (1979), *Survey Methods in Social Investigation*, Aldershot: Gower Publishing Company.

Oxfam Health Unit (1983), *Refugee Health Care, Oxfam Practical Health Guide 2*, Oxford: Oxfam.

Phillips, D. (1989), *Controlling Iodine Deficiency Disorders in Developing Countries, Oxfam Practical Health Guide 5*, Oxford: Oxfam.

Rapid Rural Appraisal Notes, available free from International Institute for Environment and Development.

Water Packs — Water Supply Scheme for Emergencies and Long Term Use. Information on the purpose, development and use of the Oxfam Water Packs, available from Oxfam, Oxford, U.K.

de Waal, A. (1989), *Famine that Kills: Darfur, Sudan, 1984 – 1985*, Oxford: Clarendon Press.

GLOSSARY

Anthropometry: Body measurements such as weight, height and arm circumference, which are used as a direct measure of an individual's nutrition and growth – their nutrition status. Collectively, the nutrition status of a population of children may be used for making comparisons over time or with other populations.

Basic food ration: A food ration that consists only of cereal grain, such as wheat or sorghum.

Body Mass Index (BMI): A numerical index of the weights and heights of adults used as a basis for making comparisons. BMI is equal to weight over height squared (weight/height^2).

Census: Includes all the people in a population in contrast to sample (see below).

Child death rate: The number of deaths of children aged 1 through 4 years per 1,000 child population of this age per year.

Cluster survey: The survey sample is based on a number of groups – 'clusters', of individuals.

Complementary ration: Food rations that improve the nutritional quality and the palatability of a basic food ration. Complementary rations may also be appropriate for use as weaning foods.

Crude mortality rate: The total number of deaths per 1,000 of the population per year.

Cut-off point: The point on a nutrition index, such as weight for height, used to categorise or screen individuals. For example children below the cut-off point of 70% WFH/L are categorised as seriously malnourished.

Dearth: Scarcity and high cost of food.

Destitution: Without any resources such as food, money or shelter.

Early warning systems: Early warning systems are designed to provide timely warnings of food scarcity in order to initiate responses that will avert famine.

Energy dense: An energy dense food has a high proportion of fat (about 20% or more), which means that it is high in energy relative to its volume and weight.

Energy requirements: WHO have recommended energy levels that are based on estimates of the energy spent on the separate processes of maintenance, growth and physical activity. Requirements therefore vary according to body size, activity, and health.

Extraction rate: The proportion of a cereal grain that remains after milling. An extraction rate of 85% is common for white wheat flour.

Food security: Food security is defined by the World Bank as 'access by all people at all times to enough food for an active, healthy life. Its essential elements are the availability of food and the ability to acquire it. Food insecurity, in turn, is the lack of access to enough food.'

Incidence: Number of new cases of a condition (e.g. cases of low birth-weight per population per year) over a specific period of time, or as a percentage of a rate (e.g. percentage of births below 2.5kg).

Infant mortality rate (IMR): The number of infant (below one year) deaths per 1,000 live births, usually presented for a given year.

Key informant: An individual in a community whose knowledge is relevant to the purpose of the survey.

Livelihood: Means of making a living – source of income.

Mean: Another term for the average, which is the total sum of all values divided by the number of values.

Nomad: Member of a tribe that moves from place to place usually with livestock looking for water and pasture.

Nutrition index: A nutrition index, such as weight for height or length, is used to compare the measurements of an individual with a group of healthy people of the same height or age.

Nutrition surveillance: The regular collection of nutrition information that is used for making decisions about actions or policies that will affect nutrition.

Nutrition survey: A nutrition survey is a 'one-off' assessment of the nutrition situation; a 'snapshot in time', which may be referred to as a cross-sectional survey

Objective: Considers facts that are not coloured by views or opinions (which are subjective).

Pastoralists: People who depend on livestock for their livelihood.

Prevalence: The proportion of population at one point in time with a condition, such as malnutrition.

Protein energy malnutrition: PEM is a range of clinical disorders that occur as a direct result of an inadequate diet and/or infectious disease. The two extreme syndromes are marasmus and kwashiorkor.

Protein energy ratio: The proportion of total energy of a food or ration that is provided by protein. (1g protein provides 4Kcal.)

Proxy indicator: An indicator that acts as a substitute for something else that is difficult to measure. For example, rates of malnutrition are sometimes used as a proxy indicator for food availability and access to food.

Purposive sampling: The selection of the sample is according to a specific purpose.

Qualitative: Qualitative methods are usually exploratory and provide background descriptive information that may be used to describe relationships between points of interest, such as malnutrition and various causal factors.

Quantitative: Quantitative methods are intended to measure the degree to which some feature of interest is present such as the prevalence of malnutrition.

Random sampling: Where all individuals or objects in the population of interest have an equal chance of being selected.

Reference population: The group of healthy children whose measurements are used for comparison with those of individual children.

Representative sample: A subset of the population that is typical of the whole population.

Screening: To test whether an individual has or has not a particular condition, for example screening for malnourished children.

Survival strategies: The ways people cope with and adapt to increasing stress on their livelihoods, caused by the effects of food scarcity and famine.

Transhumant: Seasonal moving of livestock to other areas.

Index

rapid assessment 17, 20-5, 33;
  advantages and disadvantages 20;
  diagrams 23-4; direct observation 23;
  portraits and stories 23; procedure 21;
  records 38; semi-structured
  interviews 21-2, 38; time scales 33;
  training 34-5
recipes 111-15
records 36-9: antrophometric data 37;
  other information 38-9; protein
  energy malnutrition 38;
  supplementary feeding programmes
  69; survey forms 37
reference population 6
rehydration 73
reports: format 99; writing 43-4
response options 48-51
sampling 29: bias 29; census 29;
  cluster 30-1, 80-1; interval 30;
  purposive 22; representative sample
  29; simple random 29-30
screening 66
seasonal calenders 23, 24, 25
semi-structured interviews 21-2, 38
severity assessment 10-13
standard errors 84-7
statistical methods 82-9
storage of food 116-17
supplementary feeding programmes 57,
  63-72; admission criteria 65; aims 64;
  amounts 69; closure 71; criticisms 63;
  DSM 67-8; emergency and non-
  emergency 64; follow–up surveys 71;
  food 66-7; identity bracelets 70;
  monitoring 69-70; need for 43;
  organisation 64-5; Oxfam kits 107;
  problems 71-2; recipes 111-15;
  records 69-70; screening 66; wet and
  dry rations 64
surveys *see* nutrition surveys
targeting 48, 49, 51; agency role 55;

general or universal 51, 52;
  geographical 51; limited resources
  54; selection criteria 53-4; selective
  51, 52-3; self-selection 54
telephone messages 44-5
telex 44-5
therapeutic feeding programmes 57;
  foods 73-4; monitoring 74; oral
  rehydration 73; organisation 72-3;
  Oxfam kits 107
time scales for assessments 33
training 34-6
transport 39
visits 17
vitamin deficiencies *see* deficiencies
water testing kit 108
wealth ranking 25, 78-9
weight-for-age 6
weight-for-height or length (WFH/L) 6,
  27-8
weight measurement 90
Z scores 82-3